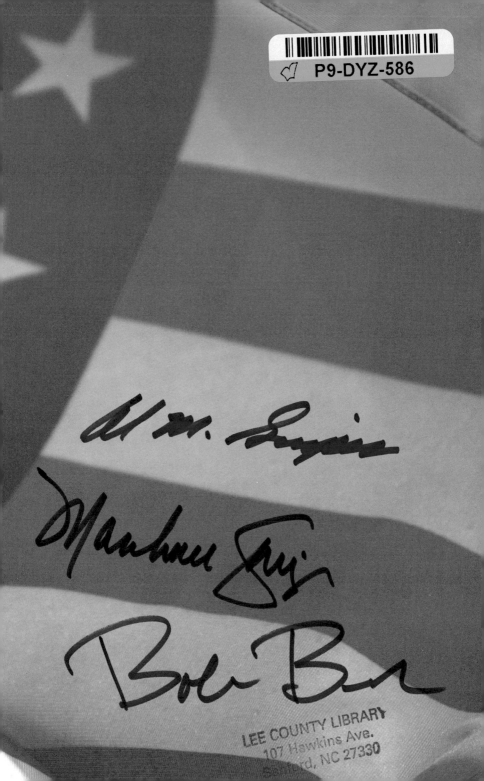

AL SNIPES

by **MARSHALL SNIPES** *and* **BOB BURKE**

Foreword by
Mickey Edwards
and
Jim Daniel

Series Editor
Gini Moore Campbell

Associate Editor
Eric Dabney

AL SNIPES

FIGHTER, FOUNDER, AND FATHER

OKLAHOMA *TRACKMAKER* SERIES

OKLAHOMA
HERITAGE
ASSOCIATION
Oklahoma City

OKLAHOMA TRACKMAKER SERIES

Printed in the United States of America.
ISBN 1-885596-53-7
Library of Congress Catalog Number 2006921776
Book cover and contents designed by Sandi Welch/www.2WDesignGroup.com

CONTENTS

DEDICATION

To Rebecca Davis Burril Snipes…
The wind beneath Al's wings for more than 51 years.

A wife, mother, mother-in-law, grandmother,
and friend to many, and role model to all.

ACKNOWLEDGMENTS

WE ARE GRATEFUL TO MANY PEOPLE for making this book happen. Carla Snipes' support and encouragement and the writing of her father's story inspired us to complete the project. The book could not have been written without Al's countless hours of interviews and reviewing old newspaper clippings, family albums, and other records. The same goes for recollections and advice from Bill Snipes and Becky Snipes Maddux, research from Brian Maughan, Mandy Snipes, and Marsh Snipes. Ben and Laurin Maddux spent much time tracking down priceless photographs of family history.

A special thanks to Mickey Edwards and Jim Daniel who have meant so much to Al over the years and for so generously writing the foreword.

We also thank so many people who consented to be interviewed for the book. They include Henry Bellmon, Frank Keating, J.C. Watts, Denzil Garrison, Jim Daniel, Marvin York, Mickey Edwards, Tom Cole, G.T. Blankenship, Joe Dodson, Charlotte Dodson, Ken McClain, Pati Thurman, Richard Lee, Curt Thompson, Jim Bowers, Brian Maughan, Tom Daxon, K.E. Smith, Dan Tipton, Grace Boulton, Don Boulton, Tom Dudley, Kay Dudley, Bud Stewart, Mel Gragg, Bob Snipes,

Mike Grady, Bill Livermon, Carolyn Snipes Gilliam Warlick, Jack McCann, Robert Nunn, Bob and Louise Mistele, Drew Mason, Robert Barcum, John O'Dell, and Isabelle McKeithen Thomas .

We are indebted to the Oklahoma Trackmaker Series editor Gini Moore Campbell and associate editor Eric Dabney, our designer, Sandi Welch, transcriptionists Debbie Neill and Shelley Dabney, and proofreaders Becky Snipes Maddux, Carla Snipes, Bill Snipes, and George and Marcia Davis.

Several organizations opened their files for research, including the Oklahoma City Community College, South Oklahoma City Chamber of Commerce, South Oklahoma City Rotary Club, Oklahoma County Republican Party, Oklahoma Republican Party, Integris Health, South Oklahoma City YMCA, and the Metropolitan YMCA.

—MARSHALL SNIPES
BOB BURKE
2006

MY CREED

I do not choose to be a common man. It is my right
to be uncommon—if I can. I seek opportunity—not security.
I do not wish to be a kept citizen, humbled and dulled
by having the state look after me. I want to take
the calculated risk: to dream and to build, to fail and to succeed.

I refuse to barter incentive for dole. I prefer the challenges
of life to the guaranteed existence: the thrill of fulfillment
to the state calm of Utopia. I will not trade freedom
for beneficence nor my dignity for a handout.

I will never cower before any master nor bend to any threat.
It is my heritage to stand erect, proud and unafraid,
to think and act for myself, to worship as I please,
enjoy the benefit of my creations and to face the world boldly
and say, this I have done. All this is what it means
to be an AMERICAN!

—AUTHOR UNKNOWN

(This creed is contained on a plaque that graced the wall of Al's office for decades. It is the creed that governs his life.)

FOREWORD

by Former Congressman Mickey Edwards

IT IS RARE THAT ONE MAN CAN PLAY A MAJOR INFLUENCE in shaping the politics of an entire state. But Al Snipes, by creating the modern Republican Party in central Oklahoma, did just that. He inherited an almost non-existent political party, organized its precincts, recruited campaign workers and candidates, and almost single-handedly built the organization that made it possible for Republicans, myself included, to win.

It is no exaggeration to say that if it had not been for Al Snipes, it is very unlikely that I would have been able to be elected to Congress or to have had the many other wonderful opportunities that have developed for me as a result of those years in office. Many people have helped me along the way, but Al has been the one indispensable man in my public service career.

Al's ability to attract, encourage, and motivate people to the cause of better government through the two-party system is a legacy that he leaves to all of us. Will Rogers once said that the mark of a great man is one who leaves this world a better place than he found it. Al Snipes is truly a "great man."

FOREWORD

by Jim Daniel

THERE ARE A FEW PEOPLE WHO CROSS OUR PATHS who have a passion that sets them apart from others. Al Snipes is one of those people. His love of and passion for his country is evident to all who know and work with him. Al feels deeply about the organizations to which he attaches himself and finds them as opportunities to assist in bettering his community and fellow man.

One of his great passions is his love for the young people of America. He believes that every child is precious in the sight of God and deserves every opportunity to reach his or her full potential. This deep conviction is borne out with his involvement in the Fellowship of Christian Athletes as well as the YMCA. I first met Al in 1965 when he came to my office on behalf of the YMCA. He was not simply raising money. He was interested in having others join him in his investment in the lives of the young people of Oklahoma City. He believed each child, regardless of color or creed, deserved the best. By stating the underlying reasons for his commitment, it was easy to respond to his challenge.

As a director of our bank, Friendly Bank of Oklahoma City, and later Banc One, Al always focused his comments on how we as a bank could help to make our community and its people better. When you asked Al to assist in a fund raising project, he always wanted to know what the outcome would be and how it would improve the quality of life of the people it touched.

Some of my fondest memories of Al were the moments when he was surrounded by children. Working with them at camp, or in a church youth group, his eyes always lit up as he saw their potential. One of my lasting memories was in the back of his Jeep at the lake while we took the young kids out for a "Snipe" hunt. Their squeals of joy and unbridled laughter made Al's day.

My life has been enriched by Al Snipes and I cherish his friendship. Hopefully, we can all touch lives and make a difference in our communities as he does.

RIGHT: Alfred Marshall Snipes, Sr., (Grandfather Snipes) in 1897 when he was eight years old.

ONE

Southern Beginnings

THE FIGHTING, FOUNDING, AND FATHERING tendencies of Alfred Marshall "Al" Snipes, Jr., sprang from his roots in Yorkshire County, England, where members of the family began appearing in official records at the beginning of the seventeenth century. The English derivation of the surname Snipes is "a small piece of land."[1]

In the decades that followed, many Snipes families left England to settle in the Virginia Colony, many by way of Barbados, the easternmost island in the Caribbean. By the middle of the seventeenth century, several Snipes families had settled in Barbados where the production of sugar, tobacco, and cotton was reliant upon the indenture of servants from the West Indies.[2]

After a generation in Barbados, the ancestral family tree of Al Snipes moved to Virginia, and eventually to the Sandhills region of what would become North Carolina, the twelfth of the original thirteen American colonies. Permanent settlement of North Carolina came late along America's eastern seaboard. After the British twice failed to establish colonies, permanent settlers began to move to the area from neighboring Virginia.

Shortly before the American Revolutionary War, William and Sarah Snipes moved to Chatham County, North Carolina. William, born in Virginia in 1735, fought in the War for Independence and furnished equipment and supplies to the Continental Army. His grave, on a farm that remains in the Snipes family, is marked by a Revolutionary War headstone. Many Snipes family reunions are held in the area.

Chatham County was named for William Penn, the Earl of Chatham, a defender of American rights in the British Parliament. The county was founded in 1771 and is located at the geographic center of North Carolina.[3]

For the next four generations, the Snipes family lived in the heart of North Carolina in Chatham County. William's son, John Manley Snipes, and his grandson, Manley, and great grandson, Charles Manley, prospered as farmers, blacksmiths, and surveyors in the fertile area. Each generation produced a number of children who became indispensable workers on the family farm.

Charles Manley Snipes, a blacksmith, made and repaired equipment for the Confederate Army in the Civil War. The Snipes were Republican, skilled with their hands, and known for their easygoing personalities. After the defeat of the South, the Snipes family continued with their lives and previous occupations.

Charles Manley's son, Alfred Marshall Snipes, Sr. (Grandfather Snipes), was born in southern Chatham County on April 4, 1889. His birth occurred in the same month that a large section of land in central Oklahoma was settled by the Land Run of 1889, land that his son, Al, would later call home.

When Grandfather Snipes was seven years old, his mother died. His older brother, John Hadley Snipes, and his wife, Lydia, moved back to help with the family farming operation and the blacksmith shop. Lydia managed the home and cared for the younger children. Family legend says that Grandfather Snipes developed a dislike for Lydia when she accused him of taking sugar.

When his father, Charles Manley Snipes, died in 1905, Grandfather Snipes moved to nearby Cameron, North Carolina, in Moore County. It is believed he worked for his older brother, Coley, who owned a lumber planing mill. The relocation was significant because the first five generations of Snipes had called Chatham County home.

Moore County was established in 1783, shortly after the end of the Revolutionary War, and was named for Alfred Moore, a famous militia colonel in the Revolution, who later became an associate justice of the United States Supreme Court.[4]

Moore County had been the scene of bloody, guerilla warfare during the American Revolution. Settlers wanted independence from Britain, but many Scottish immigrants, the Highlanders, had taken an oath of allegiance to the King of England and remained loyal to the British throne.

RIGHT: The McLaurin family in 1904. Front row, left to right, Wretha Kathleen McLaurin, Mary Alice Thomas McLaurin, Mary Ross McLaurin, James Daniel McLaurin, and Daniel Terry McLaurin. Back row, James Clarence McLaurin, Bessie Inez McLaurin, Hugh Arnold McLaurin, Annie Bell McLaurin, and Marion Conley McLaurin.

LEFT: Al's grandfather, James Daniel McLaurin, fought in the Civil War. He died the same month in 1921 that Al was born.

The town of Cameron is on land that was once part of the huge plantation of Archibald McDugald, a Highland Scot who settled in North Carolina and prospered. The town was named for Paul C. Cameron, a stockholder in a railroad that extended its line into Moore County in the early 1870s. The town was incorporated by an act of the North Carolina general assembly in 1876.[5]

The history of the Scots became important to the Snipes family story when Grandfather Snipes married Bessie Inez McLaurin, Grandmother Snipes, on December 19, 1906. The McLaurins were Southern farmers in the tradition of Thomas Jefferson and were far different than the Snipes. The McLaurins were cotton farmers and lived in a large house on their farm northeast of Cameron. They also had a house in town where they spent much time and where they lived prior to buying the farm. The McLaurins farmed for profit while the Snipes farmed primarily to feed their families. The Snipes also were involved in lumber milling, banking, farming, and bicycle and automobile repair. The McLaurins invested in the stock market and managed their farming operation.

Grandmother Snipes' father, J.D. McLaurin, had fought in the Civil War for the South. The McLaurin family remained

BELOW: Grandmother Snipes and her siblings in about 1940. In front, left to right, Mary Ross, Annie Belle, and Grandmother Snipes. Back row, T.C., Hugh, Buddy, Clarence, James Daniel, and Conley.

ABOVE: Grandfather Snipes married Bessie McLaurin in 1906. Left to right, Grandfather Snipes, Grandmother Snipes, best man Jim Gilchrist, and maid of honor, Annie Bell McLaurin, Grandmother Snipes' sister.

bitter over the Civil War when they moved to Cameron. Women family members had been treated poorly by Northern soldiers following the war. The McLaurins were Deep South in their thinking, stylish in their dress, and considered themselves "refined" Southern gentlemen and ladies.

Scottish Highlanders such as the McLaurins liked the ridges and valleys of Moore County because it reminded them of their homeland in Scotland. They easily adapted to the new land and settled along the streams to pursue their previous occupation as farmers. The sandy loam produced excellent dewberries, corn, cotton, and tobacco.

To provide a means for the farmers of the Sandhills to get their goods to market, the Highlanders oversaw the building of a plank road from Winston-Salem to Wilmington, North Carolina. The roadbed, which ran on the south side of the

McLaurin farm, was elevated in the center with drainage ditches on the side. Sills were laid on the roadbed to support the heavy wood planks laid at right angles across them. After the planks were covered with sand, they supported heavier freight wagons and swift passenger coaches. Toll houses were stationed about 11 miles apart—tolls covered maintenance costs for the road.

Then came the railroad and Paul C. Cameron, who became the richest man in North Carolina. By the time Grandfather Snipes arrived in Cameron, shortly after the turn of the twentieth century, many Scottish families had joined other farmers in the area served by the village. By 1910, the train stopped four times a day in Cameron. The town had more than 100 businesses, including a bank, several hotels, and six bars. The primary economy was supported by the surrounding farmers and the long leaf pine forests that produced lumber, tar, pitch, and turpentine for use in painting, caulking, and preserving the wood and ropes of ships.[6]

Grandfather Snipes and his wife began their family of 11 children when Pauline Evans Snipes was born on November 11, 1907, in a house believed to be across from the Greenwood Inn in Cameron. A second child, Alfred Haywood Snipes, was born on January 17, 1909. In October of that year, the Snipes home burned.

On September 24, 1910, Bessie Snipes gave birth to twins, Marjorie Lee and Mildred May Snipes. Tragically, Marjorie Lee died the following year and Mildred May died at age 11. With

Four of Al Snipes' oldest siblings, left to right, Polly, Haywood, Claire, and Mildred.

four children to support, Grandfather Snipes left his employment at his brother's mill and operated a grocery store, across the street from Greenwood Inn. He also owned a livery stable behind the Britton Hotel next door.

In 1911, Grandfather Snipes took his family to Greensboro, North Carolina, where he worked as a night watchman at the Women's College of the University of North Carolina. He also opened a bicycle repair shop on Madison Street. A fifth child, Claire Leon Snipes, was born on July 3, 1912. Also born in Greensboro was Mary Lambe Snipes, on August 17, 1914.

The family moved back to Cameron in 1916. Grace Gaynell Snipes was born on December 26, 1916. They lived in the Gady house on the McLaurin farm and helped Grandfather McLaurin care for his younger children. They also helped with

BELOW: Grandfather Snipes hired Will McNeil to work in his garage and on the Snipes farm. In this photograph, McNeil, who worked for the family for about 14 years, is shown in front of his tobacco fields in the early 1960s. McNeil's fields were adjacent to the old Snipes farm.

the farming. Grandfather McLaurin had lost his wife in 1904 and his oldest daughter in 1916.

Grandfather Snipes did not like the hard, grueling work of farming so he took a job at a Cameron auto dealership owned by his cousin, Leonard Hartsell. He was also a substitute mail carrier. At age 28, in 1917, out of patriotic feelings for his country, he registered for the draft. He never was called to active duty in World War I, probably because of the size of his family. Instead, he was sent to work in the shipyards at Norfolk, Virginia.

In 1918, Grandfather Snipes purchased a farm about a quarter mile east of the Cameron city limits. He built a home and garage that housed a small grocery store, automobile repair shop, and service station. He hired Will McNeil to work in the garage. Will's wife, Pearly, helped Grandmother Snipes care for the children.

BELOW: Al, right, at age four playing with his sister, Kitty, at home on the back porch.

Four additional children were born on the farm east of Cameron following World War I. Ernestine Faye Snipes was born April 9, 1919; Alfred Marshall "Al" Snipes, Jr. was born April 11, 1921; Valda Kathleen "Kitty" Snipes was born August 25, 1923; and Nancy Carolyn Snipes was born August 20, 1931.

Al's entry into formal education was not a pleasant one. He could not sit still and did not like the idea of spending his days within the confines of a school room. He had to repeat first grade. He constantly became embroiled in horseplay, sometimes ending in fights in the school yard. He was never mad—he just liked to rough house. Isabelle McKeithen Thomas, a schoolmate and longtime friend remembered, "My memory of Al in those early years was bloody noses and shirttails hanging out."[7] There were no school cafeterias so Al and his sisters took their lunch. His older sisters were in charge of the food and laid out a fine fare for the children each day.

In the late 1920s when Al was a young boy, the family often spent a week or so of summer vacation at Carolina or Wrightsville beach. By this time, the old plank toll road was bankrupt and no longer passable. The nearly 160-mile trip was made on sand roads that had deep ruts cut by wagons and other cars. When cars met, Al remembered, "We took one rut and the ditch and the other driver did the same. Generally, we would have to get out and help push the car back on the road."[8] Drivers could always expect two or three tire blowouts on the trip, so extra spare tires were attached to the sides of the car. Because Grandfather Snipes was a skilled mechanic, the trip to the beach took less time than for most families that found themselves stranded with broken down automobiles awaiting repair.

Life in the Roaring Twenties was good for the Snipes family. Grandfather Snipes platted his property and sold lots to develop the area. When he was not doing chores or going to school, Al enjoyed hanging around the garage where he became great friends with Will McNeil. "Will used to tell me," Al remembered, "that if I got any grease on me, he would swallow me whole. As big as his mouth was, I believed him and never got any grease on me from the garage."9

The Great Depression adversely affected the Snipes business interests in Cameron, as it did for most Americans. The Depression began with the stock market crash in 1929 and deepened as the country endured the most prolonged downturn in economic activity in modern history. The bank in Cameron closed and buildings sat vacant. Tobacco replaced dewberries as a cash crop, as dewberries had replaced pine products as the nearby forest disappeared.10

Grandfather Snipes incorrectly assumed that if merchants could extend credit for a year or so, surely the economy would rebound to near normalcy. However, after a year of providing food and car repairs on credit, he himself ran out of money. He closed the store to keep the garage open, but finally had to close the garage except for the fuel pumps. If a customer needed gasoline, Al or one of his sisters would unlock the pump to sell just two or three gallons. It was a bonus for a customer to also purchase a quart of oil, even though it might profit the business only five cents.11

By 1930 the older Snipes children had all left home to pursue educational endeavors. Haywood was in college, Polly and Claire were attending nursing school, and Mary was enrolled in beauty school.

Business worsened and Grandfather Snipes turned back to farming to support his family. He raised vegetables, grains, fruit, and livestock to feed his family and to trade to neighbors. There were blackeyed peas, corn meal, sorghum molas-

ABOVE: This is a photograph of the Greenwood Inn in Cameron in the 1970s. It is now one of many antique stores on Main Street in Cameron.

RIGHT: Al, at age eight, was already a hard worker.

ses, wheat, vegetables, and meats. There was always plenty to eat—but very little money. He raised tobacco to sell for cash but did not make enough profit to pay his fertilizer bill. With farming no longer an option, he moved his family back to Cameron in 1934 to live in the old Greenwood Inn that had become a private residence. While the family lived in the Greenwood Inn, Grandfather Snipes opened a garage in Sanford, approximately 10 miles away, and commuted. But after one year, the result was the same.[12]

For nine consecutive years, from 1931 to 1940, the Snipes farm, garage, and house were auctioned each year to pay local taxes the family could not afford. And for nine years, no one bought the farm. Each year the bid would not bring enough to pay the taxes and the property reverted to the Snipes family. As a result, it came saddled with a tax lien which Al ultimately redeemed in 1940 at age 19.[13]

The Great Depression had more than an economic effect upon Grandfather Snipes. A Mason, he also had been a member of the Cameron Baptist Church. For an unknown reason, he stopped going to church as the Great Depression ravaged his family.

Grandfather Snipes was a quiet man and never talked a great deal with anyone, including his family. Al had a curious mind at a young age and constantly asked his father questions about every conceivable subject. Grandfather Snipes told his wife that Al could accompany him on trips only if she sent someone with them to answer all of Al's questions.[14]

Grandfather Snipes was educated and read newspapers and news magazines. His interest in current events certainly was passed to Al and his siblings. He was a strict disciplinarian who only had to lower the newspaper and peer over the top if the children were getting too noisy.

Grandmother Snipes was the spiritual leader of the home. She insisted that the children attend church every time the doors were open. She also required the highest standards of behavior. She made certain her children were clean and completed their homework. She taught her children during the Great Depression that being poor was no excuse for not being clean and prompt. She also encouraged the pursuit of higher education, even though she had no idea how her younger children could afford to attend college.

In 1935, Grandfather Snipes moved his family again, for economic reasons, to a farm at Osgood, five miles from Sanford, North Carolina. The farm was owned by his brother, Frank Snipes, who was very successful in banking, lumber, coal, and commercial farming. The Snipes moved into Uncle Frank's old home place, a rambling farm house. His many barns were used to service cattle, hogs, chickens, and mules. One morning Al ran the traps and caught 14 rabbits.

At 14, Al was old enough to become a working partner with his father in the family farm. Farming was hard work from before dawn to well past dark each day. However, the financial arrangement between Grandfather Snipes and his brother made life easier.

On September 25, 1938, Grandfather Snipes traveled to Durham, North Carolina, to sell a load of tobacco. After he cashed his receipts at a local bank, he prepared to return to his home. However, two teenaged boys robbed him and hit him on the head with a bottle. The robbers dragged him into the upstairs of a nearby building, put him on a cot, and poured whiskey all over him, attempting to make it look as if he had passed out drunk.[15]

The next morning the police checked him and determined he was drunk and had been in a fight because his nose was

Al, age 17, shortly before his father was murdered in Durham, North Carolina.

bleeding. Later that night, the boys returned and hit him with an iron window weight. The following morning, the police were again summoned and officers realized Grandfather Snipes was severely injured. He was taken to the Watts Hospital in Durham where his daughter, Claire, worked. He never regained consciousness and died three days later. The two robbers were arrested, convicted, and sentenced to death. However, after a plea from their mothers, and consent from Grandmother Snipes, their sentences were reduced to life in prison. Both men died in prison.

Al, a seventeen-year-old junior at Deep River High School, had to assume responsibility to complete the harvest on the family farm. With the help of his sisters, who remained at home, and neighbors, he worked hard to keep the Snipes family together and run the farm.

RIGHT: Al's high school football team in 1940, the first fielded by Cameron High School. Front row, left to right, Horace Stone, Jim Kelly, Garland Stutts, Al, and John McDermott. Second row, Lloyd Thomas, Paul Boaz, Lawrence Cameron, Sidney Boaz, Bobby Stutts, and Luther Frank Comer, Jr. Back row, Coach M.D. Wall, Leighton McKeithen, Jim McPherson, and Murdock McKeithen.

TWO

Growing Up Quickly

Al has been very successful in keeping a good job and has been a considerable financial assistance to his widowed mother and younger sister.

—**R.F. LOWRY,** PRINCIPAL
CAMERON HIGH SCHOOL

AFTER **G**RANDFATHER **S**NIPES' **DEATH** and with Al leading the effort, the Snipes family farm yielded a good crop in 1938. The tobacco harvest brought fair prices as the Great Depression's grip on the American economy waned.

In early 1939, Grandmother Snipes and her children moved back to Cameron and rented a house near the Greenwood Inn, just west of the new post office. There was enough money remaining from the sale of crops to provide for the family for sometime.

In the summer of 1939, following his junior year, Al went to Atlanta, Georgia, to live with his sister, Pauline, and her husband, Ernest Hafling. Al landed a job at Rosenthal's sheet metal shop where he earned 30 cents an hour. He saved enough money to ensure that his mother and three sisters, Kitty, Grace, and Carolyn, would have proper food and clothing for the winter. Other siblings helped as well.

Al wanted to play football his senior year in high school, but the Cameron school system did not have a team. Al and his best friend, Murdock McKeithen, convinced the principal to allow a team to be formed if all parents would sign a waiver releasing the school district from liability for any injuries suffered by their children. The district made it clear that the money for uniforms had to be raised and was not provided for in the school budget.[1]

Al and Murdock, with the encouragement of Murdock's father, L.B. McKeithen, Sr., collected the signed waivers and raised money necessary for team uniforms—great organizational training that would benefit Al later in life. It was only six-man football—but it was football, and Al was anxious to play.

Prior to the final game of the season, one of Al's legs became infected. His condition was so bad that he was afraid he would not be allowed to play. However, Al was so determined to play that he told no one about his condition. He saw action for 57 of the 60 minutes of the game. The next day, he underwent surgery to remove the infection.

Al also played varsity basketball and was named to the second squad of the all-county team. His propensity for a rough style of play caused him to foul out of many games. Once, because of car troubles, Al did not arrive at the site of a game until the beginning of the second quarter. Even so, he fouled out before halftime.

Cameron High School did not have a gymnasium so practices were held on outside clay courts. Basketball became Al's favorite sport, although he also lettered in football and baseball. Always one for the dramatic, Al hit his first and only home run in baseball during his last plate appearance as a senior.

Al was known as "Marshall" throughout high school. He was popular with other students and was the only one with a car. In fact, his car, a 1934 Chevrolet four-door sedan he had purchased with money he had earned, served as the team bus for the Cameron sports teams.

It was in high school that Al began to develop an interest in government, politics, and world affairs. He began reading newspapers and would literally jump over the furniture to listen to Walter Winchell's commentary when it aired on the family's radio. Al began listening to politicians and liked what he heard from Republicans. He tried to convince his mother to vote for Republican presidential nominee Wendell Wilkie in 1940. However, his mother was a lifelong Democrat and probably never voted for a Republican. Al believed his parents' votes canceled out each other.[2]

Al graduated from Cameron High School in May, 1940. Living in the area was relatively inexpensive because the town had never recovered from the Great Depression. Only a hand-

ful of businesses remained from the more than 100 that existed before the economic downturn.

Following high school graduation, Al never considered working locally because there were no jobs. He traveled to Washington, D.C., to live with his brother, Haywood and his wife, Laure. Haywood helped Al obtain a job. Al sent enough money back to his mother to support the family. It was common for the Snipes children to send financial support back to the family in Cameron. Other siblings helped some, but most of them were struggling in the Depression to support their own families. By 1940, only Al's sisters, Carolyn and Kitty, remained at home.

LEFT: The Cameron High School basketball team in 1939-1940. Front row, left to right, Lloyd Thomas, Jim Kelly, Bobby Stutts, Garland Stutts, and Al. Second row, Paul Boaz, Roy Cooper, Sidney Boaz, Haywood Bunnell, and Murdock McKeithen. Third row, Wade Gaddy, Talmedge Clayton, Luther Frank Comer, Jr., and John McDermott. Back row, Clayton Cameron, Talmedge Clayton, and Coach M.D. Wall.

BELOW: The Snipes family at about the time of Al's graduation from Cameron High School in 1940. Al is on the far right.

In the fall of 1940, Al moved back home to Cameron and worked at Fort Bragg, North Carolina, before moving on to Newport News, Virginia, where he took a job with a construction company. Germany

RIGHT: Al was always a fast driver. However, this time, the night caught up with him as Al's vehicle is about to be towed to the repair shop.

had invaded Poland and the smell of the coming world war was in the air. Al remembered, "Anyone who was paying attention knew it would not be long before America was drawn into the conflict."[3]

Jobs were plentiful in Newport News because the buildup for war was intense. Al was employed as a carpenter building sub-floors and roofs for much needed housing. Using his newly learned skills as a carpenter, Al returned to Washington, D.C., and went to work in nearby Baltimore, Maryland, building apartment houses.

When the Baltimore job was completed, Al heard about the availability of great jobs. The federal government was building the Pentagon, the new home for America's military agencies. To work for the construction company building the Pentagon, union membership was required. Al was denied membership in the union as a carpenter because he was only 20 years old, a year below the minimum age the union placed on such positions.[4]

Not to be denied just because of his tender age, Al took the suggestion of the superintendent of the construction job and reapplied for his union card wearing a hat and with a few days' growth of beard. It worked—he was hired. Because Al was told he had to join a labor union, it was an experience so distasteful that it gave him a lifelong dislike of unions. He recalled, "I was incensed. I was not about to go to work for someone I had been supervising in the past. Merit did not seem to matter to the union—only age, seniority, and job protection."[5]

Al was a tough boss. His workers were non-productive. One afternoon, his crew was so unresponsive to his demands, he fired them all. When he sought new workers from the union steward, a heated exchange of words followed. The contractor bowed to the steward's demands and Al was removed from his supervisory duties. He was tired of the union and frustrated with Democratic national politics. He thought the country was moving toward socialism under the New Deal policies of President Franklin D. Roosevelt.[6]

Al got another bad taste of Democratic politicians when he heard allegations that former Oklahoma Congressman Will Rogers, who had been defeated in his bid for reelection, had been placed in charge of rationing gasoline stamps and was bootlegging the stamps on the side. Rogers was a school teacher in Moore, Oklahoma, who ran for office on the popularity of the other Will Rogers, Oklahoma's favorite son, the humorist and movie star, who had been killed in a plane crash in Alaska in 1935. They were not related to each other.

Al at work constructing the Pentagon in Alexandria, Virginia. The huge complex would become home to America's military command.

There was a personal angle to the Congressman Rogers' controversy. It was rumored that one of Al's friends was buying some of the stamps. Al never knew whether or not the charges were true, but the allegations were distressing, especially as the country prepared for certain involvement in World War II.

In spite of the whirlwind happenings in the world, Al immersed himself in his job. He worked every possible hour his supervisors would allow—he worked two shifts many days and occasionally three shifts per day. In 1940, with his earnings, and after sending money home to his mother, he purchased a 1939 Chrysler from his sister Claire. She later enlisted in the United States Army as a nurse. While in the Army, she met and married Jake Lyons in early 1942. Jake was shipped out to North Africa where he served under General George S. Patton throughout the European campaign of World War II.

A 1941 Chrysler on loan from Claire to Al in front of the sign at the edge of nearby Pinehurst, North Carolina. Note the sign advertising a famous resort for $10 a night. The hotel was the host hotel for many of golf's famous tournaments, including the 2005 U.S. Open.

PINEHURST
HOTELS NOW OPEN
MINIMUM RATES WITH MEALS

THE CAROLINA FROM $10.00 WITH MEALS

THE BERKSHIRE $5.00 TO $6.00 WITH MEALS

By the middle of 1941, it was apparent to Al, and most of the citizens of the country, that America was going to war. Al, like most red-blooded young American males, was anxious to enlist and fight for his country. He unsuccessfully tried to join the Army Air Corps, the Navy Air Force, and the SeaBees. He failed to pass the military physical because of an old finger injury. A childhood accident had left his right hand index finger slightly crooked. However, he was accepted as a member of the Civil Air Patrol and was ordered to report for duty on December 16, 1941.[7]

Two weeks before he was to begin active duty, the federal government froze manpower levels and Al's induction into the Civil Air Patrol was canceled. Al continued to work at his construction job and closely followed developments in the war in Europe and the Pacific.

Finally, in January, 1943, after nearly two frustrating years of trying, Al was drafted for limited service in the United States Army. Because he had initially failed his physical, he was allowed to serve in the Army with duties limited to non-combat roles. He was anxious to fight and was promised that he could apply for removal of the limited service designation after 90 days.

He was assigned to the Army's induction station at Fort Bragg, North Carolina, where he supervised the process of inducting from 500 to 2,000 new soldiers each day. After 90 days, his request for reclassification was again denied, partly because he had done such a good job organizing the induction station. His commander did not want him to leave.[8]

Al was classified as a carpenter and also supervised the making of furniture for base offices. His main job was to organize inductees for work in the shops. However, he was increasingly frustrated by the commanding officer's repeated denials of his requests for reclassification. His relationship with his commanding officer deteriorated. When Al refused to give priority to make a specific piece of furniture for the commander, he was placed under house arrest. Al was suspicious that some of the furniture was being taken home for personal use by some of the officers. He told the first sergeant and the adjutant that if he was ever arrested, he would request an investigation into where the furniture was going. He was told to go back to work.[9]

Al's real military service began when he was finally accepted by the Army Air Force in August, 1943. His acceptance was made possible by continued efforts of L.B. McKeithen, local Cameron businessman, R.F. Lowry, principal of Cameron High School, and his sister, Claire, who was a nurse at the base at Fort Bragg and was influential with members of the medical examining board.

McKeithen, also a member of the local school board, wrote about Al, "He has been very successful in keeping a good job and has been a considerable financial assistance to his widowed mother and younger sister. Marshall [Al] is of the aggressive type and I believe you will find him well fitted by temperament for this kind of work."[10]

In his letter of recommendation, Lowry called Al a distinguished graduate of Cameron High school, "He is a fine all around young man who possesses that rare courage and fine muscular coordination which should make him a splendid aviation cadet. We feel that you will not go wrong in this young man."[11]

Al got the scare of his life two days before his Air Force orders arrived when the first sergeant—Al believed it was done for spite—informed him he needed to take a physical to prepare him as a member of a hospital evacuation squadron that was

Al stands beside his aircraft during flight training at Beavers Falls, Pennsylvania. On the day of this photograph, the temperature was 0 degrees Fahrenheit.

headed overseas. However, his Army Air Force orders arrived in time to save him from overseas duty in the hospital unit.

The old Army Air Corps' name had been changed to the Army Air Force six months before the beginning of America's involvement in World War II. As war approached, Secretary of War Henry L. Stimson and Army Chief of Staff George C.

Marshall saw the need for a stronger role for Army aviation. Consequently, they created the Army Air Force with General H.H. "Hap" Arnold at its head. However, because of the aura attached to their command's former name, many World War II veterans still refer to their service in the Army Air Force as time spent in the Army Air Corps.[12]

After basic training in Greensboro, North Carolina, Al was assigned to a facility at Beavers Falls, Pennsylvania, to complete two years of college credit required to enter the cadet program. The Army had a surplus of pilots and standards were continually raised to limit the number of cadets in training.

While in Pennsylvania, Al obtained his pilot's license—but not without fanfare. During the last 20 minutes of training before he could solo, he was taking off with an instructor by his side. When the aircraft reached 350 feet, the engine blew and Al was forced to make an emergency landing in a snow-covered corn field. The deep snow absorbed much of the shock of the landing, surely sparing his life.[13]

In 1944, World War II was winding down and the Army sent 50,000 aviation cadets back to the infantry. Fortunately, Al survived the cut and was sent to aviation school at Keesler Field in Biloxi, Mississippi. He was a pilot, but was assigned to a reserve pool. There he was retrained as a mechanic at the base which was the home of the B-24 Liberator mechanic training squadron. Only then did he sadly recognize that he would probably never fight in the war effort.

Al's commander at Keesler encouraged his troops to take part in the base boxing program. It was common knowledge that members of the boxing team were given special privileges. Al, who loved to box since his days in elementary school, decided to try out for the team. He was impressive in tryouts and made the team. Boxing was popular, both on the base and in the surrounding city. Friday night fights promoting the sale of war bonds drew huge crowds.

While making the team was relatively easy for Al, staying on the team was difficult. Boxers had to pass rigorous physical tests and continually defend their positions on the team. The fights were considered amateur, but eight ounce gloves were used and headgear was not allowed—the same standard as a professional fight.[14]

One morning while performing situps, Al passed the 450 mark, prompting his instructor to ask him if he thought he could surpass the Army record of 1,357 continuous situps. Al accepted the challenge and stopped only after he passed the record.

Al looked forward to his weekly fights at Keesler, dubbed by *The Ring* Magazine as the "Army's center of boxing." Many professionals of that era were stationed and fought at Keesler, including former world welterweight champion Fritzie Zivits, Jimmy Braddock, Benny Leonard, Jimmy Bivins, and Billy Conn.

The Ring Magazine applauded the boxing program at Keesler:

> The men are toughening their muscles in a comprehensive program of competitive sports to ready themselves physically for the fight against Axis bullies. They are learning to use their fists, as well as their brains and Uncle Sam's planes, to beat a victory tattoo against the military chins of Hitler and Hirohito.[15]

Al's first big match at Keesler was in front of 8,000 spectators against base champion and local favorite James Cecil. Al won the fight. The base newspaper reported, "James Cecil dropped his middleweight crown to PFC Al Snipes, for his last local ring appearance. Cecil disappointed his fans by placing caution above aggression. He held the challenger at bay in the first period, but Snipes accumulated a good margin of points in the latter two rounds for the evident verdict."

For most of 1944, Al fought weekly at Keesler Field. His record was 21-1. In his one loss, he was hit by his opponent's elbow and suffered a cut that stopped the fight. Al later beat the same fighter in a rematch. Newspaper stories of his boxing matches described his "roundhouse rights" and "solar plexis" punches that carried him to victory. After one fight, the reporter wrote, "PFC Snipes opening his meeting with PFC Miller with a burst of blows that confused the latter into a nine-count fall before a KO at 1:30 of the first round."

The highlight of Al's boxing career at Keesler was winning the Gulf States Golden Gloves Championships. Al's boxing career was on its way.

RIGHT: Al trained many hours each day as a member of the boxing team at Hendricks Air Force Base in Sebring, Florida.

THREE

The Main Event

He's terrific! You watch him! He'll tear their heads off!
—Chief Parris

THE MORE **AL** BOXED, THE BETTER HE FOUGHT. In 1945, he was transferred to Hendricks Field in Sebring, Florida. At Hendricks, he trained as an airplane mechanic and enjoyed the privileges of being on the boxing team.

Later, Al was placed in charge of the permanent base officers' physical training and coached the Hendricks Field boxing team. Every time Al's boxing team was ready for a good fight program, his soldier-boxers were transferred to other duty stations. After all, there was a war on.

Al's record remained strong. He lost only one of 22 fights at the base and became a crowd favorite because of his aggressive style. Al's superiors realized he was fighting a losing battle trying to revive boxing at Hendricks because the base was not large enough to support a boxing program.[1]

Most of Al's fights were in base programs where as many as 1,500 patrons would attend weekly fights. However, he and his team also entered Golden Gloves tournaments. Even in defeat,

Al was cheered by the fans. After he lost a bad decision in a Fort Myers, Florida, tournament to determine who would fight in the EFTC championships in Alabama, the base newspaper sports reporter wrote:

> When the hand of Snipes' opponent was raised in victory by the referee, the huge crowd booed and hooted the decision. There was no doubt in their mind that Al was the winner by a big margin, and they gave the Hendricks ringman plenty of moral support with their long sustained shouts of protest.

That Snipes was the victim of a bad decision was evidenced when the officer handed Al the trophy—an act that started the fans cheering.[2]

When the cheering ended, fans began showering the ring with debris. Al and his trainer were afraid of injury and left the ring. Outside, Al learned that his commander had bet his opponent's commanding officer $200 on the fight. The other commander obviously knew Al won the fight and handed $200 to Al's commander who promptly stuffed the $200 in Al's boxing trunks.[3]

The next day, the commander of the base where the fight occurred reversed the decision and Al was made the official winner. He was chosen to represent Florida in the Eastern Flying Training Command (EFTC) tournament, equivalent to the Army Air Force championship. Ironically, the championship trophy presented to Al from that fight is the only boxing trophy he kept—the others were given to friends.[4]

Al was flown on a B-24 aircraft to Maxwell Field, Alabama, for the EFTC fights. In the semi-finals, Al scored an upset technical

Al, back row second from right, and members of the Hendricks Air Force Base boxing team. The two trophies in front of Al were given to him for the Fort Meyers tournament championship and the sportsmanship trophy. It was the only sportsmanship trophy Al ever won.

ABOVE: Al holding the championship trophy won at the EFTC tournament at Fort Myers. After the judges awarded the victory to his opponent in an obvious miscarriage of justice, the decision was overturned the following day by the commanding officer of the base where his opponent was stationed and the championship trophy was given to Al.

Al's official Army Air Force photograph.

knock out (TKO) win over local hero, Billy Fallon, with a terrific right hook in the second round. Fallon was considered one of the classiest middleweights and was the favorite to win the tournament.[5]

In the finals, Al fought Jerry Miller, a professional fighter from Smyrna Field, Tennessee. After Al had beaten Fallon in the semi-finals, he became the favorite to win the championship. However, in what local newspapers described as "a wild swinging affair," Al lost a close decision to Miller.[6] Al thought he won the fight over Miller who had more than 850 fights, had been trained by Fritzie Zivits,

LEFT: Al liked anything that would go fast, especially his motorcycle that he had for pleasure at Hendricks Air Force Base in 1945.

and was named outstanding boxer of the EFTC because of his defeat of Al.

A month later, Al traveled to Miami, Florida, to enter the Florida Golden Gloves championship. There, he defeated Bill Pocza in the 160-pound middleweight class for the Florida Golden Gloves championship.

World War II finally ended with the surrender of the Japanese. Al was given the option to be discharged early or remain in physical education and be transferred to Japan where American troops were helping rebuild the war torn land. Al wanted to go home because he had not been able to do any-

One of the few photographs that exist showing Al during Army Air Force boxing action. This photograph was taken during Al's match with Bill Pocza in the Florida Golden Gloves championship.

thing except teach officers and other airmen physical fitness.

In early 1946, Al was transferred to Smryna Air Force Base, Tennessee, for separation processing. He officially separated from the Army on February 15, 1946, at Fort McPherson in Atlanta, Georgia. However, his discharge did not come without some last minute excitement.

On his last night in the Army, he spent the evening on the town with a nurse he had met and dated on a previous trip to Georgia in 1939. During the evening, Al had an encounter with a military policeman over a uniform violation. It was resolved the following morning without incident and Al was granted an honorable discharge.[7]

Al headed for North Carolina on a bus with money in the bank he had saved prior to joining the Army Air Force. His first priority was to buy an automobile, a difficult purchase because they were being sold at a premium following the end of World War II.

For $850 Al purchased a 1939 Ford two-door coupe from his brother-in-law, Charles Clodfelter. The car had been used as a North Carolina state highway patrol car and had an oversized engine and a bullet proof windshield. In the new car, Al visited friends and family all over the southeastern United States from Georgia to Washington, D.C. His family had scattered from their North Carolina roots. His sister, Pauline, was in Florida; Kitty was in Georgia; Claire was in Japan; and

Mary was in Massachusetts. His brother, Haywood, lived in Missouri. His sisters Grace and Carolyn, and Al's mother, had moved to Oklahoma City, Oklahoma. Only Faye remained in North Carolina.

Like so many recently discharged veterans, Al was anxious to chase the "American Dream". He was restless and wanted to devote his full attention and energy to a career—although he frankly did not know which career he would follow. He was a hard worker and fully confident he would return to North Carolina.[8]

Less than a month after Al was discharged from the military, he decided to visit his mother in Oklahoma City. In early 1945, Al had loaned his sister, Grace, and her husband, Herb Moore, $3,750 for the purchase of frozen food lockers to supplement their grocery store business in the Capitol Hill section of Oklahoma City. Frozen foods were becoming popular and a new business of renting frozen food lockers sprang up across the nation.

Al's intention was to collect the money owed to him, move back to North Carolina, get a job, buy some land, build a mortgage-free house, get married, and start a family. The events of the next few weeks changed his plans—lucky for Oklahoma.

Al found the situation "a mess" in Oklahoma City. His mother and brother-in-law were both ill and bedridden. The grocery store, Herb's Super Market, at 2828 South Robinson Avenue, and frozen food locker business were in terrible shape. Due to poor management, many customers had lost confidence in the operation. The frozen food locker business was disorganized. Grace was trying to manage the store, care for her sick husband and mother, her five-year-old son, and Al's youngest

sister, Carolyn, a student at Capitol Hill High School. The entire family lived in a three bedroom, one bath apartment above the grocery store.[9]

Al was concerned for his family, so he decided to stay a few months to help Grace run the business. After all, building the business was the only way he could ever get his money back.

Al moved into the apartment and began working long hours at the grocery store. After a few weeks, he and Grace were able to turn the store around. Customer confidence improved and the business began showing a profit.

Knowing how much Al enjoyed boxing in the Army Air Force, Herb encouraged him to get back into boxing, a popular sport in Oklahoma City following World War II. Boxing enjoyed more coverage in the sports pages of Oklahoma City newspapers than University of Oklahoma football. Major professional fights on radio had promoted the sport to high levels as fans began attending amateur fights. Especially popular in Oklahoma were Golden Gloves boxing tournaments.

Golden Gloves boxing had begun in Chicago, Illinois, in 1928, as a charity event sponsored by the *Chicago Tribune*. Ten years later, in 1938, Bus Ham, sports editor of *The Daily Oklahoman*, promoted the first Golden Gloves tournament in Oklahoma City to benefit the Ice and Milk Fund, a charity that provided milk and ice for children and disabled citizens who were not recipients of local and federal relief programs.[10]

Amateur boxing flourished in the 1920s and 1930s in Oklahoma. G.M. Byerley, considered the father of amateur boxing in the Sooner State, along with Dude McCook, Harry Gilstrap, Eugene "Chief" Parris, Charles Saulsberry, Jimmy Taylor, Claire Gans, and Dale Palmer, promoted matches among teams around the state. Early bouts were fought at the Coliseum at the Oklahoma City Stockyards, the arena at the Farmers Market, and the Municipal Auditorium. It was common for more than 1,000 boxing fans to pay to see weekly fights.[11]

On March 16, 1946, Al visited the Oklahoma City Boxing Club at the Municipal Auditorium to watch other boxers work out. Al's brother-in-law, Herb, told Chief Parris, the famous coach of the boxing club, about Al's success in the ring in the

Army Air Force. Herb and Parris convinced Al to get into the ring and workout with one of the local boxers. Parris thought it would give him an opportunity to look at Al's skills.[12]

What Al did not know was that the boxer in the ring was training to turn professional later that spring. However, after Al easily controlled the action with his challenger for a few rounds, Parris announced he wanted Al to be his middleweight on the Oklahoma City Boxing Club team that was preparing to fight in the state Amateur Athletic Union (AAU) championship at Anadarko three days later.[13]

With only one workout under his belt, Al won his first two fights at the tournament over Fred Ebich of Stillwater and Eddie Lara of the Riverside Indian School team. Wally Wallis of the *Oklahoma City Times* called Al the "surprise package" of the tournament, writing, "Snipes, just out of an army uniform, uncorked the biggest upset of opening night by winning a split decision from Fred Ebich."[14] Another reporter called the match "the wildest kind of a fight" with Al getting "the nod because of a straight left to the chin that floored Ebich midway through the third round."[15]

Al lost in the finals to Enos Anquoe of Anadarko, although Al later avenged the loss with a TKO over Anquoe in a rematch. With Al's help, the Oklahoma City Boxing Club made a huge splash in the state tournament against gifted Native American boxers from the Fort Sill Indian School, Riverside Indian School, Anadarko Boxing Club, and Concho Indian School.[16]

Quickly, Al won three more fights in the spring of 1946 at Golden Gloves bouts in Okmulgee and Ardmore, Oklahoma, and Wichita, Kansas. Boxing was again in Al's blood—largely due to the encouragement of Chief Parris, a legend in Oklahoma boxing circles. Parris liked Al and told a newspaper reporter, "He's terrific! You watch him! He'll tear their heads off!"

FIGHT PROGRAM

2nd Annual
Oklahoma A A U
Boxing Tournament

ANADARKO, OKLAHOMA

★

MARCH 19, 20, 21, 22, 1946
Bouts Start at 8 P. M.

★

Tournament Sponsored by
Anadarko Chamber of Commerce
and American Legion Post No. 24

Parris, of Irish and Cherokee descent, had a reputation as a fighter by the age of 14 in Allowee, Oklahoma. By age 17, he was fighting professionally, knocking out larger and older opponents at carnivals and fairs. He turned professional and was Southwest Champion in the welterweight class, won a championship tournament in California, and even beat the champion of Mexico in 1937. He won 220 of his 227 professional fights.[17]

After his retirement from boxing, Parris began helping troubled youngsters in Oklahoma City, training them in a small garage behind the Exchange Avenue fire station. Many of the young boxers used the skills learned from Parris to earn college scholarships.[18]

Parris used a distinctive hands-on approach to train Al. Al was just out of the Army, cocky, and frankly did not cherish the thought of following orders from Parris, or anyone. During one bout with a left handed fighter, Parris yelled at Al from the corner, "If you don't throw your right hand, you're walking home!" Al responded and knocked out his opponent.[19]

On another occasion, Al did not like Parris' instructions and told the ex-fighter, "Where I come from, you don't tell a man what to do, you show him!" Parris, much heavier than Al, promptly entered the ring and gave Al a six-minute lesson in how to "listen to your coach." From that moment on, Al listened to Parris.[20] Although boxing was again at the top of Al's list of priorities, he continued to work 12 to 16 hours a day in the grocery store. The long hours cut short his opportunity to train, but he still believed he could make the grocery store successful and recover his debt.

The fight program for the March, 1946, AAU boxing tournament at Anadarko, Oklahoma.

Living in an apartment with five other people became impractical. In the early summer of 1946, when it became apparent that

A newspaper cartoon echoed the popularity of boxing matches in the 1940s at Oklahoma City's Municipal Auditorium. Boxing was bigger than University of Oklahoma football.

he would not be leaving Oklahoma City anytime soon, Al purchased a duplex at 720 Southwest 31st Street. Herb, Grace, and son, Duke, lived on one side, and Al, his sister, Carolyn, and Grandmother Snipes lived on the other.

After the long summer of work, Al decided to enter the Golden Gloves Jamboree in Oklahoma City in September. He had not worked out during the summer, but Chief Parris needed a middleweight who could compete on a national level. Parris called Al "the best middleweight he had ever seen." Al somehow found time to train at the Downtown Gym after a full day at the store. Using what little spare time there was, he fine-tuned his skills for the Jamboree.[21]

Chief Parris, left, and Al at a reception for Parris given by his former boxers in 1989.

Boxing was not the only fight Al had on his hands. As manager of Herb's Super Market, Al was active in the Oklahoma Retail Grocers Association. In the fall of 1946, the store was among 86 Oklahoma grocery stores chosen by the Teamsters Union for secondary picketing. Teamsters were upset because Al and other grocers sold DeCoursey milk, produced at a non-union dairy. Al was mad and believed picketers were outside their rights to stand with signs in front of his store and harass

Al, always the promoter, advertised price cuts and drew large crowds of customers to the grocery store.

his customers. Al often became embroiled in verbal battles with union members.[22]

With a distaste for unions from his experience as a carpenter in Washington, D. C., Al helped hire attorney George Miskovsky to halt picketing of grocery stores. The ploy worked when District Judge Albert C. Hunt enjoined the union from picketing the stores in October, 1946.[23] It would not be the last time Al would raise his voice against union activity.

After Judge Hunt made his ruling, the union changed their tactics with Al. Union members began parking outside the grocery store and followed him everywhere, trying to intimidate him. For awhile, Al carried a gun for his own safety. One day, Al had enough. The union men followed him to downtown Oklahoma City where he was headed to make a bank deposit. At the busy intersection of Park and Robinson avenues, Al used the jam of the rush hour traffic to make his move. He stepped from his car and approached the vehicle that contained the union members.

Still in prime physical condition, Al opened the driver's side door and a colorful verbal exchange ensued. Al told the men, "You've been threatening me. It's time to get out and put up or shut up." Al, standing in the middle of the street, dared the men to touch him, but they would not get out of their car. Meanwhile, motorists honked their horns and a crowd gathered, cheering Al on. As sirens blared from a

ABOVE: Al, his coach, and his Oklahoma City Boxing Club teammates in 1946. Left to right, Coach Chief Parris, Al, Herschel Acton and Robert Nunn prepare for the Mid-South championship in St. Louis, Missouri.

police car arriving at the scene, Al told the union men to never follow him again. He never saw them again.

Al turned his full attention to boxing. During the next 52 days, Al and the Oklahoma City Boxing Club caught fire. Harold "Red" Andrews, veteran ring official, called the 1946 Oklahoma City Boxing Club team the greatest team in Oklahoma history. Fighting to raise money for the Ice and Milk Fund, 31 of Oklahoma's finest Golden Glovers fought in the Jamboree at Oklahoma City's Municipal Auditorium.

RIGHT: A poster from a 1946 fight between Al and Bud Bledsoe, billed as the "main event."

Al was cheered on by his sister, Carolyn, friends, Bob and Louise Mistele, his sister, Grace, and her husband, Herb, and Grandmother Snipes.

Welterweight Herschel Acton, the nation's top-rated amateur lightweight the previous year, highlighted the card at the Jamboree, although Al soon became a favorite of the 3,800 fans

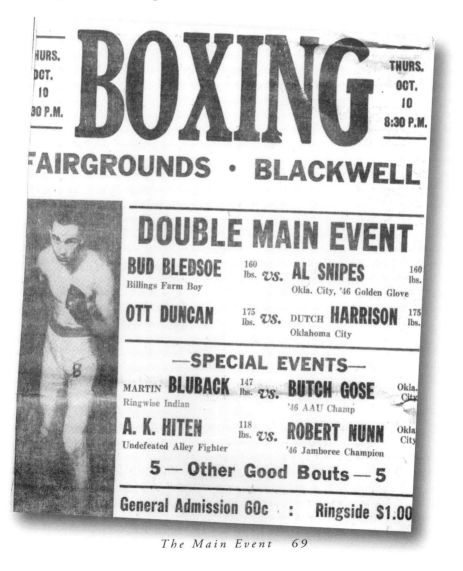

BOXING

THURS. OCT. 10 8:30 P.M.

THURS. OCT. 10 8:30 P.M.

FAIRGROUNDS · BLACKWELL

DOUBLE MAIN EVENT

BUD BLEDSOE 160 lbs. *vs.* **AL SNIPES** 160 lbs.
Billings Farm Boy   Okla. City, '46 Golden Glove

OTT DUNCAN 175 lbs. *vs.* DUTCH **HARRISON** 175 lbs.
Oklahoma City

—SPECIAL EVENTS—

MARTIN **BLUBACK** 147 lbs. *vs.* **BUTCH GOSE** Okla. City
Ringwise Indian   '46 AAU Champ

A. K. HITEN 118 lbs. *vs.* **ROBERT NUNN** Okla. City
Undefeated Alley Fighter   '46 Jamboree Champion

5 — Other Good Bouts — 5

General Admission 60c : Ringside $1.00

who jammed the arena. In a preliminary bout, Al beat Horace Tahbone of Anadarko. Then, in the championship bout, Al scored the only knockout of the tournament, defeating Bobby Horn of Sand Springs, Oklahoma, who won the state novice crown in 1945. Reporter Pete Rice wrote, "Snipes shot a straight right to the head of Horn and sent him to the floor in 44 seconds of the final frame."[24]

Al was nearly unbeatable in September and October, 1946. In addition to the Golden Gloves Jamboree, he won his weight class at the Tournament of Champions in St. Louis. He won six matches and two tournaments by knock out, TKO, or unanimous decision. No longer was Al an unknown fighter—he had become a main event.

Al had one more fight before he retired from the ring, at least the first time he retired. Without any chance to train because of work at the grocery store, Al lost a heartbreak decision to hometown fighter Kenneth Beavers of Lawton in a contest at Cameron University in Lawton, Oklahoma. Al pushed Beavers all over the ring and never dreamed he lost the fight. As the newspaper reported, "Snipes lost on a split decision after the Oklahoma City battler carried the fight to the expressionless Beavers all the way." But, as sometimes happened in the world of boxing, the nod went to the hometown boxer.

At age 25, Al was a gifted fighter with a brilliant future. His fights were a manifestation of his talent and an element of his character. He was described in many newspaper articles as "handsome, good-looking, the best 160-pound prospect in years, Capitol Hill grocer, a puncher, an infighter, part of a two-fisted crew,

Al, left, fighting in the Golden Gloves Jamboree at the Municipal Auditorium in Oklahoma City. The referee is Harold "Red" Andrews, later a longtime member of the Oklahoma House of Representatives.

a champion, and butcher boy." He also was called by Jack McCann "a man of steel" and one of the all-time greats of Oklahoma City boxing.

Al considered his options. Dewey "Snorter" Luster, the former University of Oklahoma (OU) football coach, was promoting an OU boxing team and OU officials expressed interest

in Al and other fighters on the Oklahoma City Boxing Club team. Others urged Al to turn professional and try to earn a living fighting as a welterweight. However, Al believed boxing might lose its popularity as a sport as OU football began its rise to national prominence. And, he had a business to run, so his love for boxing had to take a back seat to reality.[25]

BELOW: Grandmother Snipes, Bessie Inez McLaurin Snipes, lived in North Carolina most of her life. She is buried alongside her husband and five of her children in the cemetery in Cameron, North Carolina.

ABOVE: Al's brother, Haywood, was his mentor and had a significant impact on his life. Haywood attended Duke University, North Carolina State University, and graduated from Catholic University in Washington, D.C. He was an architect and lived for many years in Poplar Bluff, Missouri.

RIGHT: Rebecca Davis was a strong young woman. Between the age of 14 and 20, she lost her mother, a close friend in a tragic automobile accident, and her first husband. Those events occurred during a time when most young girls were thinking about parties and dating. Rebecca also spent her senior year in a body cast due to a broken back.

FOUR

KO'd by Cupid

Where there is love—there is life.
—MAHATMA GANDHI

SINCE ARRIVING IN OKLAHOMA CITY, Al had attended church and later joined Capitol Hill Baptist Church with his mother and sisters. At a church function he met Bob Mistele who played for the Oklahoma City Indians, the top farm team for the major league Cleveland Indians.

Mistele had been an exceptional college athlete in both baseball, as a pitcher, and football, as a quarterback. He spent the war years playing professional baseball with the Chicago White Sox. Because of his religious conviction that he should not work on Sunday, he negotiated his contract with the White Sox that allowed him to not pitch on Sundays.

When major leaguers who had been called to active military duty returned to their teams after World War II, Mistele was

This photograph of Bob and Louise Mistele appeared in *The Daily Oklahoman* as Bob was leaving for spring training with the Oklahoma City Indians. *Courtesy Oklahoma Publishing Company.*

demoted to the minor leagues—that is how he ended up in Oklahoma City in 1946. He and Al, because of their intense love for sports, became fast friends. Together, they attended local sporting events and church functions. Mistele was an enthusiastic young man and an accomplished storyteller. When someone would ask him if Al was a great boxer and if he won fights, Mistele would say, "Is the Pope Catholic?"[1]

Mistele attended several of Al's fights and described his new friend as "a tough cookie" and a "nifty fighter." Al's admiration of Mistele as an athlete was reciprocal. He enjoyed watching him pitch for the Indians at the Texas League Ballpark in downtown Oklahoma City.[2]

In December, 1946, Mistele thought Al was working too hard and needed a girlfriend to spice up his life. After church on a Sunday night, he set up a dinner date for Al and Rebecca Davis Burril at Beverly's Restaurant, a popular spot of high society in the capital city.

Rebecca was a war widow. In 1943, while living with her sister Margaret, she met Leslie Auburn Burril, a Mississippian assigned to Navy training in Norman, Oklahoma. While Leslie was on liberty, he visited Capitol Hill Baptist Church and fell in love with Rebecca. After a short courtship, they were engaged. Leslie was shipped out for further training in San Diego, California.

Rebecca wanted to go to college, but settled for business school because of the long commute to the University of Oklahoma in Norman. Rebecca completed courses at Hill's Business University and worked for awhile before Leslie sent for her. They were married on October 16, 1943.

Rebecca became a secretary for the Navy Department Labor Board as Leslie prepared to enter active overseas duty. After a December, 1944 trip to see relatives in Mississippi, Leslie took a train back to San Diego for assignment overseas. Rebecca boarded another train to Oklahoma City, not knowing they would never see each other again.[3]

Leslie was assigned to Patrol Bombing Squadron 102 that flew PB4Y aircraft, also known as the B-24 Liberator. As a gunner on the plane's top turret, he was on his 24th mission on May 9, 1945, when the aircraft came under heavy anti-aircraft fire from Japanese-held Marcus Island, an isolated island in the northwestern Pacific Ocean. The plane crashed into the sea and there were no survivors. Ironically, Al had worked as a mechanic on the B-24 Liberator when he was stationed at Keesler Field in 1944.[4]

In the following days, the Navy notified Rebecca that Leslie was missing in action. She was not prepared for the bad news—her husband had been in combat for only two months. The words of the Navy telegram were straight and to the point:

THE NAVY DEPARTMENT DEEPLY REGRETS TO INFORM YOU THAT YOUR HUSBAND LESLIE AUBURN BURRIL, AVIATION MACHINISTS MATE SECOND CLASS, IS MISSING FOLLOWING ACTION WHILE IN THE SERVICE OF HIS COUNTRY.[5]

Leslie did not remain on the missing in action list long. On June 3, 1945, a second telegram came with the devastating news:

THERE IS NO HOPE FOR HIS SURVIVAL. HE HAS LOST HIS LIFE AS RESULT OF ENEMY

ACTION...SINCERE SYMPATHY IS EXTENDED
TO YOU IN YOUR GREAT SORROW.

VICE ADMIRAL RANDALL JACOBS,
CHIEF OF NAVAL PERSONNEL[6]

Rebecca was devastated. She was widowed one month before her 21st birthday—losing her husband just three months before the war ended with the atomic bombing of the Japanese cities of Hiroshima and Nagasaki.

Rebecca, left, and her best friend, Louise Lowery Mistele, were both war widows. In 1945 they took a vacation by train to New York City and both declared it was a trip of a lifetime.

After spending time with Leslie's family in Mississippi and Louisiana, Rebecca returned to Oklahoma City where she lived with her sister, Margaret, and her husband, Ed Hardin. Margaret discouraged discussion of Leslie's death and encouraged Rebecca to move on with her life. Rebecca obeyed her sister's leading and never talked about Leslie's death until she wrote a book about that portion of her life nearly 50 years later.

Rebecca was still reeling from Leslie's death 19 months later when she met Al Snipes in December, 1946. She had seen him at Capitol Hill Baptist Church for months, but they had never been formally introduced. With Bob Mistele trying to be "cupid," the dinner with Rebecca and Al came off perfectly. In early 1947, Al asked Rebecca for three dates, but Al almost did not ask her out for a fourth occasion because she was so shy and obviously was not over the death of her husband.[7]

Perhaps because both Al and Rebecca had endured hardships in their teenage years, their relationship was destined for success and happiness. Al had never seriously dated anyone else, partly because he believed spending too much time with girls would draw his attention away from his goals of buying land and building and paying for a house before he was married. He still dreamed of building a home, and a life, on a certain piece of land north of Southern Pines, North Carolina. He remembered, "Dating someone more than once or twice would jeopardize that goal." However, Rebecca was different. Al was attracted to her because of her strong Christian character and the fact that she seemed so "special."[8]

This photograph, the Snipes family favorite, was taken of Rebecca just before she married Al in 1947.

It was difficult for the romance to flourish in the spring of 1947 because Al was given the opportunity to build a frozen food locker plant in Wilburton, Oklahoma, nearly four hours from Oklahoma City. After the war, modern day refrigerators were not available to store frozen food in homes. The next best thing was for customers to rent lockers in a frozen food plant and store food there until it was needed in the home. Lockers filled the gap between the advent of frozen food and in-home refrigerators with freezing units.

In May, 1947, the Wilburton project was completed and Al returned to Oklahoma City. Even though he was working 70 to 80 hours a week at the grocery store, he found time to date Rebecca. Their dates consisted of going to church and seeing an occasional movie or eating at local restaurants. Their two favorite restaurants were Beverly's on North Lincoln Boulevard, the site of their first date, and Bishop's Restaurant, in downtown Oklahoma City across the street from the Huckins Hotel. Both restaurants later became customers of Al's frozen food locker business.[9]

Soon, Rebecca and Al began falling in love and discussing marriage. Al was hesitant, solely because of finances. The grocery store was not doing well and he pushed his brother-in-law, Herb, to put it up for sale. Al was optimistic that someone would buy the business and he could finally be repaid the money he had loaned Herb and Grace years before. However, the business never sold and eventually Al became the owner.

Al discovered that Herb's attorney had never perfected Al's mortgage on the property and business and that another creditor had first rights to any proceeds from the sale of the property. Al simply had no recourse on his mortgage. To compound the financial problems, Herb traded the frozen food locker plant in Wilburton for a couple of farms. Al was frustrated, even though Herb raised his salary from $45 to $55 a week. Still loyal to the success of the business, Al never took his full salary, only taking money he needed to live on.[10]

Al tried everything to make the supermarket a success. As post-war retail prices skyrocketed on consumer items, Al joined other merchants in rolling back prices on groceries. The Newburyport plan swept the nation's retailers with promises of an across-the-board discount. The front windows on Herb's Super Market—later the name was changed to Al's Super Market—announced a ten percent discount on all meats and groceries. The price cut was welcomed by consumers, but the additional volume produced short-term success at best.

In August, 1947, Al overlooked his financial woes and proposed to Rebecca in the driveway at Ed and Margaret Hardin's house at 326 Southwest 44th Street. Rebecca said "Yes!" and their engagement was made public in *The Daily Oklahoman* on August 24.

In the meantime, some of Al's friends encouraged him to stop working 12 to 16 hours a day to salvage the grocery store and return to boxing. After pressure from Chief Parris and several of his old teammates, Al decided to enter the 1947 Golden Gloves Jamboree and defend his title. Although Rebecca was less than excited about boxing, she attended the Jamboree only after Al promised her that this would be his last time to box, a promise he kept. Al's appearance in the 1947 Jamboree was the only time Rebecca ever saw her husband compete in the ring.[11]

Sports fans who paid attention to the boxing news on the sports page of Oklahoma City newspapers would never have known that Al had retired the previous year. The build up for the Golden Gloves tournament was huge. Boxing writer Pete Rice in *The Daily Oklahoman* wrote, "Snipes missed the tail end of the 1946-1947 season because he held to his job so closely, but he is working hard in preparation for the upcoming battle."[12]

In the days before the tournament, Al was mentioned in nearly every boxing story in local newspapers. He was referred

Al poses for a promotional picture with the boxing trophies for the 1947 Oklahoma Golden Gloves Jamboree. This photograph in *The Daily Oklahoman* was part of pre-fight publicity. Al won his weight class the previous year but lost in the finals in 1947 when his right arm was broken. He finished the fight, but lost his only fight by unanimous decision. *Courtesy Oklahoma Publishing Company.*

to as part of the "cream of Oklahoma's Golden Glove crop." Pete Rice promoted the lineup of fighters, "You'd better take your adding machine if you're gonna keep track of the titles that are carried into the Auditorium ring Monday night when the fastest field in history battles for honors in the fifth annual Golden Gloves Jamboree…Al Snipes, last year's Jamboree King of the middleweights is back."[13]

The Municipal Auditorium was packed with 2,500 boxing fans on September 1 when Al, with a slicing right hook, opened a cut over the left eye of opponent Evans Anquoe at 1:38 of the second round. With little training, Al had won a major boxing victory in the Golden Gloves Jamboree tournament.[14]

The ten month absence from the grind of training and a broken arm cost Al the championship in his final bout in which he faced Bobby Horn of Sand Springs. Horn was the same young man Al had beaten in the title fight in 1946. This time, Al's arm was broken in the first round of the contest. He did not tell anyone, even though he had little use of the arm for the balance of the fight. In the end, he suffered the only unanimous loss of his career.

The local newspaper announced Al's retirement from the ring with a simple headline—"Kayoed by Cupid," referring to Rebecca. Al's boxing career was over—but fighting never left his blood. Rebecca had accomplished something no fighter ever had.

Al had a remarkable four-year career of more than 60 wins and only 6 losses. He won five of eight tournaments he entered, lost in the finals of two tournaments, and semi-finals of the other. He won Golden Gloves titles in Florida, Oklahoma, and the Mid-West Championships in St. Louis, Missouri, and Army championships while stationed at both Keesler and Hendricks fields.

RIGHT: Al holds hot checks presented by customers at the grocery store. On one occasion, Al, still in great shape from his boxing days, chased a man who had given him a fraudulent check and made a citizen's arrest on the sidewalk six blocks away. The incident was reported in the local newspaper. *Courtesy Oklahoma Publishing Company.*

FIVE

The Struggle

When fate is adverse, a wise man can always strive for happiness and sail against the wind to attain it.

—ROUSSEAU

REBECCA WORKED AT THE **V**ETERAN'S **A**DMINISTRATION office and Al labored at the grocery store as wedding plans came together. They were married on November 30, 1947, at Capitol Hill Baptist Church, with Reverend Hugh Bumpass officiating. Rebecca's sister, Billie Ruth Davis, was the maid of honor and Al's brother, Haywood Snipes, was the best man.

The wedding was a happy time for all involved. Grandmother Snipes, two of his sisters, Grace and Carolyn, and two brothers-in-law, Jake and Herb, attended. Rebecca's father and stepmother, James and Vivian Davis, and her niece, Jerry Turner, also were present for the wedding.

LEFT: Rebecca and Al were married on November 30, 1947, at Capitol Hill Baptist Church in Oklahoma City.

BELOW: Left to right, at the Snipes' 1947 wedding, Grandmother Snipes, Al, Rebecca, Rebecca's father and stepmother, James and Vivian Davis. Mr. and Mrs. Davis lived in Nashville, Tennessee.

ABOVE: Rebecca and Al having dinner on their honeymoon at the Baker Hotel in Dallas, Texas.

RIGHT: Rebecca and Al shortly after they were married in 1947. They were visiting Al's sister, Claire, in Lawton, Oklahoma.

Al and Rebecca began their family on October 1, 1949, with the birth of their first child. The baby was named Alfred Marshall Snipes, Jr., the same legal name as Al. There is an explanation for that oddity. Al and Rebecca wanted to name the baby after his father and grandfather, but were uncertain if he should be a "Jr." or the "III." Even though the baby was technically the third, he was given

Rebecca was completely supportive of Al trying to salvage the grocery store.

the legal name Alfred Marshall Snipes, Jr. From his earliest years, he was called Marshall, so there was no confusion among family members.[1]

At the time that Marshall was born, Al and Rebecca lived in the guest house on Lloyd Bartlett's farm at 601 Southwest 59th Street. Approximately one year later, they moved to Southwest 59th Street and Blackwelder Avenue and Grandmother Snipes and Carolyn moved in with them.

The following year, Al, Rebecca, and Marshall moved to 214 Southwest 28th Street across the street from the grocery store and next door to Jim and Joy Young. Grandmother Snipes and Carolyn moved to Atlanta, Georgia, with Herb and Grace.

Al always enjoyed playing with his children. Here he holds Marshall high in the air. Note Marshall's "Al's MKT" tee shirt, advertising the grocery store.

In 1951, the Snipes moved to 1321 Kinkaid Drive in Rancho Village, the newest area in Capitol Hill and one of the first tract-home additions in south Oklahoma City.

A second child, William Ray Snipes was born on November 29, 1952. The final child was a cheerful baby girl, Rebecca Louise "Becky" Snipes, born on July 14, 1954. Becky was named after her mother and her mother's best friend, Louise Mistele.

From the time Al arrived in Oklahoma City in 1946, his life could be described as a struggle. On one hand, he had a wonderful life—a happy marriage, three children, and eventually a career in insurance. However, the grocery store was a financial burden for many years. By 1946, two Humpty

BELOW: Becky on her first birthday.

RIGHT: Becky Snipes when she was two years old.

Al, left, prided himself in stocking a great variety of fresh fruit and vegetables in the produce section of Al's Market.

Dumpty, two Safeway, and three large independent grocery stores were located within one half mile of Al's store. Price wars were frequent—profit margins were slim. In the early 1950s, the store and frozen food locker plant suffered from a devastating fire, disrupting business and further placing a burden on Al.

By 1953 Al knew it was time to get out of the grocery business. After all, he had entered the arena only to collect a debt. He sold the store and took back a note to secure the sale.

He then used the note as collateral to borrow money from Oklahoma National Bank to pay all his creditors. Lloyd Bartlett had been Al's banker and friend from church since Al arrived in Oklahoma City. He was Al's mentor from the early days in Capitol Hill and became a lifelong friend.

After nine months, the store buyer quit paying installments on the note and was deep in debt with suppliers. Al made what later proved to be a bad decision to take back the grocery store. The store was in serious trouble—the buyer had run up payables, depleted the inventory, and lost customers. Further, sales were down and competition had increased. Traffic had increased on Robinson Avenue but the store was not convenient to workers stopping for groceries on their way home.

Creditors were impatient and the store was forced into involuntary bankruptcy in 1955. Faced with mounting pressures, Al decided to close the store and concentrate on the frozen food locker business. It took Al five years, working 12 to 14 hours a day to recover from his losses.[2]

Al was embarrassed. He had come to Oklahoma and worked 70 to 80 hours a week to make the store profitable. Even though the creditors were being paid, the stigma of failure would have a lifelong positive effect. It was from that failure that Al learned the lessons that would make him a successful businessman in later years.

After the store closed, Al looked for a job. He wanted a career—and he found it in the insurance industry. In 1955, he went to work in the Farmers Insurance sales program and became an insurance agent. He knew everyone in Capitol Hill and believed he could be successful in the insurance business. From the Farmers' office at Southwest 28th Street and South Western Avenue, Al began making cold calls.

Because of the financial strain, the Snipes family took no vacations and there was no money above basic living expenses. The only trips the family took were occasional visits to Lawton, Oklahoma, to visit Al's sister, Claire, her husband, Jake, and their four children, Sarah, Barbara, Charles, and Carol.

No matter how hard Al worked, he made time for his family. Together, he and Rebecca provided a secure and loving home for their three children.

From childhood, the Snipes children remembered their mother always being at home with them. Al came home for dinner every night, but usually returned to work. Rebecca did not like to leave her children with babysitters and planned her life around the children.[3]

Daughter, Becky Snipes Maddux, remembered, "If politics and civic projects were Dad's forte, then the home was Mom's. She was probably one of the most creative, resourceful people I have ever known."[4] Rebecca could, and would make almost anything. She sewed most of the children's clothing, Halloween costumes, choir robes, curtains, pillows, and dustruffles. Her creations were beautiful and never looked "homemade."[5]

Grandmother Snipes with her children at a family reunion in 1951. Front row, left to right, Al, Claire, Grace, Haywood, and Kitty. Back row, Faye, Grandmother Snipes, Carolyn, Polly, and Mary. It was the first of many reunions in Cameron, North Carolina that continue today.

Rebecca went the extra mile to make the lives of her children

RIGHT: Becky, left, and Bill at a piano recital. Bill was dressed rather formal for the athlete that he was.

Bill, left, and Becky, look as if they had just gotten away with something.

Bill, left, Marshall, and Becky were the focus of their parents' efforts to raise them in the right way.

special. If a cousin came to spend the weekend with Becky, her mother would arise early and spend the morning sewing matching pajamas—a little girl's dream. She made things for school projects and sewed purses for many of Becky's friends. Whatever the current fashion craze was for girls, Rebecca was on top of it.[6]

She never missed a little league game, was a Cub Scout den mother, a Sunday School teacher, a choir mother, a home room mother, and, together with Al, took the family to church at Capitol Hill Baptist three times a week.

Rebecca's life revolved around her family and church. She and Al were youth group leaders and taught Sunday School at the church. She made certain the children attended little

ABOVE: The Snipes were a classic Ozzie and Harriet family. The children participated in scouting programs, little league, and church activities. At this Cub Scout meeting for Marshall, the entire family was present. In the background are Al, Rebecca, Bill, and Becky.

RIGHT: A frequent meeting place for the Snipes family was the home of Aunt Myrtle Hutchinson, a cousin to Ed Hardin, Rebecca's brother-in-law. Aunt Myrtle was famous for her home cooked meals. Left to right, Rebecca, Ed Hardin, Aunt Myrtle, and her daughter, Evelyn Hutchinson Caldwell.

league practices and swimming and piano lessons, bringing organization to the busy lives of the three children. She made sensible decisions of prioritizing her children's activities. Once she refused twirling lessons for Becky when twirling for little girls was popular, insisting that sticking with piano lessons would pay more worthy rewards later in life.[7]

Al was involved in Rotary Club in 1950. The first Rotary project he worked
on was to help build a float for a parade on Commerce Street in Capitol
Hill. Al is third from right on the front row. Note his informal dress—he
was managing the supermarket while most of his fellow Rotarians worked
desk jobs in Capitol Hill businesses. On Al's right is Lee DesCamps.

Extended family was significant in the developing years of the Snipes children. Rebecca's sister, Margaret, and her husband, Ed Hardin, had no children and served as surrogate grandparents for Marshall, Bill, and Becky. Ed was a successful oil and gas executive with Champlin Oil Company. Ed's cousin, Myrtle Hutchinson, was a widow who lived on Commerce Street and served many Sunday meals for the Snipes and Hardin families in her home.

While Rebecca was keeping the home fires burning, Al was making a living and becoming interested in the affairs of the community and world around him. Al's brother-in-law, Ed Hardin, was a founding member of the Capitol Hill Rotary Club, now the South Oklahoma City Rotary Club, and asked Al in 1949 to become a charter member. Al also organized and coached the Capitol Hill Baptist Church basketball team and sponsored and coached the Al's Supermarket softball team

In 1950, Al met an equally energetic and hard working optometrist named K.E. "Doc" Smith, who expressed an interest in bettering the community. Doc and Al formed a friendship with a mutual desire to work selflessly. Nearly every institutional advancement in south Oklahoma City for the next 55 years would benefit from their leadership. The "Old Guard" leaders of Capitol Hill were not progressive and were seemingly content with the status quo—but not Doc and Al.

Capitol Hill was like a small town across the Canadian River from downtown Oklahoma City. The small developed area stretched roughly from Shields Avenue on the east to Western Avenue on the west and from Southwest 23rd Street to Southwest 44th Street.

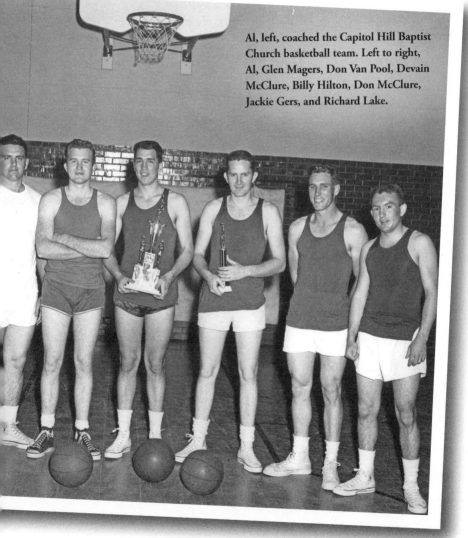

Al, left, coached the Capitol Hill Baptist Church basketball team. Left to right, Al, Glen Magers, Don Van Pool, Devain McClure, Billy Hilton, Don McClure, Jackie Gers, and Richard Lake.

Commerce Street, the heart of the community, was a thriving commercial district. The Hill included Oklahoma National Bank, Capitol Hill Savings & Loan, Capitol Hill Baptist Church, Capitol Hill Methodist Church, Langston's, J.C. Penney, John A. Brown, Sneed's Furniture, several movie theaters, Howard Brothers Florists, Hunter Funeral Home, Capitol Hill Funeral

ABOVE: Becky, left, and Bill at Camp Classen.

RIGHT: The Snipes children in 1956. Left to right, Becky, Marshall, and Bill.

Home, Kress Department Store, Katz Drug Store, Sears, Roebuck, & Co., OTASCO, Capitol Hill Bakery, and many other small businesses. *The Capitol Hill Beacon* was the local newspaper and was the lifeblood of communication on the Hill.[8]

Commerce Street was important enough for President Dwight D. Eisenhower to appear in a parade there in the 1950s and presidential candidates Richard Nixon and John F. Kennedy campaigned on the sidewalks of the area in 1960. The bus stop at Commerce and Robinson provided easy access to downtown Oklahoma City. The area was crowded with

Al's historic office at 3215 South Western Avenue in Oklahoma City. The office was a converted house that served as headquarters for many GOP candidates and petition drives.

shoppers and children playing on the sidewalks. Parades on Saturdays and holidays drew huge crowds. Al remembered, "Everyone knew everyone. The streets were safe and life was relatively simple."[9]

About the time Al became involved in community affairs, Dodson's Cafeteria opened on Commerce Street. Until Dodson's opened, there was not a nice place to eat in Capitol Hill. Joe and Charlotte Dodson and Joe's parents, Ben and Ruby Lee Dodson, operated the cafeteria in the basement of the building that housed Langston's and John A. Brown. Many leading citizens warned them that a cafeteria could not be successful in the area. The Dodsons proved the critics wrong—the cafeteria was open for 48 years.[10]

Al and Doc Smith played a role in the opening of Dodson's Cafeteria. Before the facility opened for business, Al and Doc, a self-appointed committee of two, welcomed the Dodsons to Capitol Hill and predicted the cafeteria's success. Charlotte Dodson recalled, "Al introduced himself to us and then he introduced us to everyone he knew in Capitol Hill. He reached out to everyone and we fed him a thousand times."[11]

The Snipes, Bartletts, Dodsons, and Smiths became lifelong friends. The cafeteria was the gathering place for the business community. Al continued to tirelessly and relentlessly work in his insurance business, in volunteer activities at church, and for anything that would make life better in south Oklahoma City.

In 1958, Al became an independent insurance agent. He joined Frank Fisher, Jules Dubois, and Bob Carroll in converting Al and Rebecca's previous residence at 214 Southwest 28th Street into an office. Fisher, Snipes, Carroll and Dubois Insurance Agency was formed and operated from that location until Al split off and formed his own agency in 1960. He secured a contract to sell policies for Aetna Insurance Company and his agency began to flourish. In 2006, Al's son, Bill, still owned and managed the agency.[12]

In 1960, Al purchased an office building at 3215 South Western Avenue, a location that became historic as the future home of many activities of the Oklahoma County Republican Party, campaign headquarters for numerous Republican candidates, including the famous Vondel Smith shoe box campaign, the first office of South Oklahoma City Junior College, and official district office of Congressman Mickey Edwards. State Senator Jimmy Birdsong had an office in the building, as did Marshall Snipes. It was quite a history for a converted nondescript house that contained approximately 2,400 square feet.[13]

In 1960, Doc Smith was elected chairman of the board of directors of the Capitol Hill Chamber of Commerce and made the building of a hospital in south Oklahoma City a priority.[14]

With Al and Rebecca's help, Smith conducted a door-to-door campaign to raise private money to build South Community Hospital, now Integris Southwest Medical Center. It was the first civic project in which Rebecca was involved. Until that time, she had focused her energy on raising three children. But the idea of having a hospital close by to serve her family and friends was appealing.

After the hospital was built, a battle over control of the hospital ensued. A lawsuit was filed and an election was required to affirm the decision of the district court in favor of the governing board. Al successfully ran the campaign from Doc Smith's office. Later, Al was elected to the board of the hospital's foundation, a position he held until 2004.

By 1960, Al had recovered from his losses on the grocery store and frozen food locker business, had successfully entered the insurance business, and, for the first time since he came to Oklahoma 14 years earlier, began to breathe a little easier.

RIGHT: Al posed with Judy the Elephant, a popular attraction at the Oklahoma City Zoo, to publicize the October 22, 1953 visit of Congressman Charles A. Halleck. The elephant was the GOP symbol and Judy was happy to pose with Republican activists.

SIX

Getting Involved

*All that is necessary for the triumph of evil
is for good men to do nothing.*

—EDMUND BURKE

ACTIVE INVOLVEMENT IN POLITICS CAME NATURAL to Al. It began with his insatiable desire in high school to learn more about current events. His experience with the labor union in Washington, D.C., and his concern over socialism creeping into the American way of life, heightened his awareness of what was going on in elections and government at all levels.

Al strongly believed in right and wrong. His fighting nature mandated that he stand up for what he believed—even if he was the only one standing. Additional brushes with unions in his grocery store business in south Oklahoma City made him aware of the importance of grassroots politicians. He also was influenced by one of his customers, Mary Vanderwoort, the only active voice in the Republican Party in south Oklahoma City. She would follow Al up and down the aisles of the grocery store talking politics and urging Al to become active as a Republican.

It took little encouragement from Mrs. Vanderwoort to get Al involved. He believed the Democratic administration of President Truman and his post-war policies were moving the nation in the wrong direction. He also believed that both the federal government in Washington, D.C., and the state government of Oklahoma were filled with dishonesty and were non-responsive to needs and desires of the people. Oklahoma, Al said, would never move forward if politics as usual, controlled by the "good old boys," continued.[1]

Al joined the Young Republicans in 1951 and backed Republican presidential nominee Robert A. Taft, a United States Senator from Ohio and son of former President William Howard Taft. Al was impressed with Taft's conservative views on many subjects, especially labor law. Al heard Taft talk about the unfair advantages that unions had in collective bargaining. Because of Al's local experiences with unions, he agreed with Taft's views. Taft was a sponsor of the landmark labor legislation, the Taft-Hartley Act, designed to create equity in collective bargaining between labor and management.[2]

After Taft won several early primaries, General Dwight D. Eisenhower entered the presidential race. Eisenhower, with huge popularity from service in World War II, rapidly moved ahead of Taft. At the Republican Convention in Philadelphia, Pennsylvania, in July, 1952, Eisenhower was selected to carry the GOP banner against Democratic nominee, Illinois Governor Adlai Stevenson. Eisenhower selected Richard M. Nixon of California as his running mate. The Taft-Eisenhower split was the first conservative-moderate split in the Republican Party.[3]

As a confirmed conservative, Al preferred Taft's views on national government, but quickly fell in step with the Eisenhower candidacy. He knew he supported the Republican Party's national platform that called for smaller government and less taxes on the backs of the American people. Al became involved in the presidential campaign in Oklahoma County, handing out bumper stickers and campaign buttons that said, "I Like Ike." Eisenhower took the high road in the campaign, promising to go to Korea and end the impasse of the war in that country, while leaving the political attacking to vice presidential nominee Nixon.[4]

Al won a contest sponsored by the Young Republicans by signing up the most new members. The prize was $350 to apply to the expenses of attending Eisenhower's inauguration and related gatherings in January, 1953, in Washington, D.C. Al added his own money and he and Rebecca made the trip, an exciting time as Eisenhower, the war hero, began leadership of the United States. Al, who had lived and worked in the nation's capital years before, was in awe of the inaugural ball held in the McDonough Gymnasium at Georgetown University and the inaugural parade that he watched in front of the White House.

When he returned to Oklahoma City, Al was determined to build the influence of the Republican Party in Oklahoma. The two-party system was non-existent in the Sooner State for the first half of the twentieth century. The state never had a Republican governor or lieutenant governor and an overwhelming majority of other statewide and local offices were held by Democrats.

All of Oklahoma was overwhelmingly Democratic—particularly the rural areas which dominated Oklahoma politics. For much of the state's history, the rural domination made sense because that is where a majority of the population lived. However, Oklahomans moved from the farm to the cities, primarily Oklahoma City and Tulsa, during World War II and the years that followed. Many left to find work during the war—and stayed.

Even with the population shift, Democrats and rural legislators continued to wield all the power in state government. The state constitution mandated that the legislative districts created for members of the State Senate and House of Representatives reflect the population and that future legislatures should redraw the districts after each federal census. Rural legislators wanted to maintain their power and failed to reapportion the legislature for 50 years.

By the 1950s nearly half the state's population lived in the areas surrounding Tulsa and Oklahoma counties, although the two large counties still had only two seats in the State Senate and a handful of seats in the House of Representatives. On election day, a voter in sparsely populated Beaver County in the Oklahoma Panhandle carried as much weight as 80 citizens of Oklahoma County.[5]

Against the backdrop of overwhelming Democratic control, Al went to work. He was a tireless worker in filling the void of leadership in Oklahoma County and across the state.

He buttonholed businessmen, teachers, and anyone in south Oklahoma City who would listen to his plea for help to elect Republican candidates.

Al worked tirelessly to recruit candidates—an effort that was the toughest part of Al's job. With overwhelming Democratic registration, finding Republicans to run against entrenched Democrats in districts with huge Democratic majorities were very tough, but Al never stopped trying.[6]

The leader of the country, President Eisenhower, was a Republican and had won Oklahoma's electoral votes in 1952. But GOP influence in Oklahoma was scarce at best.

Al had two things going for him—a fighting spirit for what he believed in and a familiar face. His Golden Gloves fights had resulted in his photograph regularly appearing on the sports pages of Oklahoma City newspapers. He was a hero to thousands of fight fans who would listen to his arguments about why they should be active in the Republican Party.

Al was a visionary and believed he could work hard to achieve the desired results. When Republicans held no statewide elective offices and only 20 percent of the seats in the legislature, Al believed that someday Republicans would rule the state. He was right.

Al found that the fledgling Republican Party in Oklahoma barely existed. There was no major grassroots organization, no serious program to recruit potential candidates, no permanent headquarters, no party newspaper, and no money. In fact, the entire records of the county party structure fit in one small folder and included approximately $2,700 in unpaid bills.

County courthouses were Democratic and controlled the election process—Republicans were on the outside looking in. But Al saw the mood of Oklahoma voters, and the country as a whole, become more conservative.

When Republican leaders came to town, Al was in the midst of the publicity surrounding the visit. When House Majority Leader Charles A. Halleck of Indiana appeared at a GOP function in Oklahoma City, Al's photograph appeared in the newspaper, standing in front of an elephant, the Republican Party symbol. Al helped organize Halleck's visit to speak to more than 100 well-wishers at a birthday celebration for President Eisenhower.

Al believed he could reach more people for the Republican cause in mass meetings rather than convincing them one at a time over coffee. He pushed membership in the Young Republicans Club and promoted meetings with special speakers. In 1954, he organized the largest meeting ever of Republicans in the Capitol Hill section of Oklahoma City. Al told a reporter, "The Hill is now pretty well organized. We want to have good government out here by giving Capitol Hill a two-party system."[7]

It was not easy work to convert Capitol Hill to a two-party system. The south side of Oklahoma City had long been a blue collar area and tended to be heavily Democratic. However, as national Democrats were viewed as more liberal, conservative Oklahoma working people switched their allegiance.

Vote totals in elections since 1948 showed that more voters were casting their ballots for Republican candidates than ever before. In fact, before 1948, Oklahoma County had a higher percentage of Democratic voters in seven of ten presidential elections than the remainder of the state. Beginning in 1952, Oklahoma County Republicans showed their muscle by getting out a higher percentage of GOP voters than the rest of the state.[8]

Oklahoma's Republican Party was dominated by leadership of northern Oklahoma oilmen until the middle of the twentieth century. Jim McGraw and Lew Wentz of Ponca

Al worked with the Secret Service on many details surrounding President Eisenhower's visit to Oklahoma City in 1957. He helped organize a parade in downtown Oklahoma City and through Capitol Hill. *Courtesy Oklahoma Publishing Company.*

City and W.G. "Bill" Skelly of Tulsa served as national committeemen for decades. Historian Mary Lu Tracewell Gordon called this period of party history the "personal party era." She wrote, "It was the era when the state Republican Party leaders kept the party in their own hands and discouraged any new growth."[9]

Until the 1950s Oklahoma City Republicans offered little resistance to the domination of the party by the oilmen. However, with the election of Eisenhower, political patronage meant jobs and positions of power. Oklahoma County wanted its share of the spoils of victory. Lew Wentz died in 1949 and new Republican leaders, such as Al, wanted to offer their skills to direct the party's future.[10]

Oklahoma County had difficulty raising as much money as Tulsa County for the national Republican Party but Oklahoma County Republicans, led by Al and others, began a grassroots campaign that added members to the GOP fold monthly. Al was very active in Eisenhower's reelection campaign in 1956. Oklahoma County voted more Republican than ever in sending Eisenhower back to the White House for a second term.

By the late 1950s Al had grown in popularity with Oklahoma County Republicans and was elected county chairman at the convention on January 30, 1960. Phyllisjean Morris was elected county vice chairman. Al had been hesitant about running for county chairman but agreed to serve. He was certainly prepared to take on the job. He was ward chairman from 1952 to 1958 and was the county organization coordinator for the two years before he was elected chairman.

After his election, Al said his first objective as chairman of the Republican Party in Oklahoma's largest city and county was to make the county a two-party county, essential, in his thinking, to good government. He told reporters that he was sure

Al was chosen as sergeant-at-arms for the 1958 Republican State Convention. Al, right, confronts a union picketer outside the convention in Oklahoma City. *Courtesy Oklahoma Publishing Company.*

there were enough people in the county who wanted good government to welcome the two-party system and support it.[11]

Al attended the Republican National Convention in 1960 in Chicago as an assistant doorkeeper. It was his first of five national conventions.

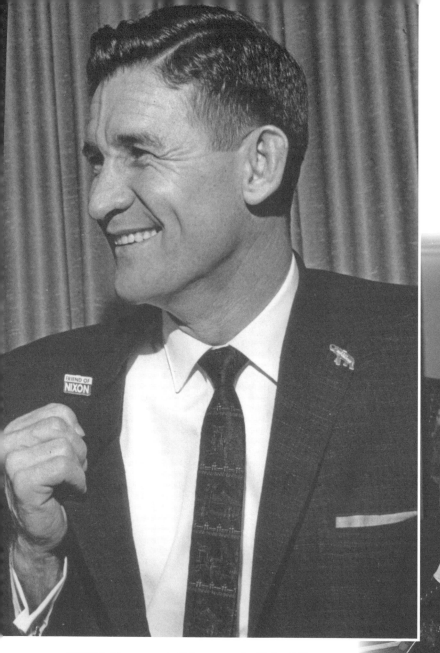

ABOVE: Al was proud of his support for Richard Nixon in the 1960 presidential election, displaying his "Friend of Nixon" button. *Courtesy Oklahoma Publishing Company.*

BELOW: On the eve of the 1960 general election, GOP campaign work-
ers make last-minute calls to drum up support for the Nixon-Lodge ticket.
At left is Phyllisjean Morris. In the center, on the telephone, is Henry
Bellmon. Al is at right.

Al became vocal, early and often, about the candidacy of former Vice President Richard Nixon in the 1960 presidential race. Schools were set up to train campaign workers to take the Republican message door to door. Al said, "We fully intend to visit every voter in the county before election day."[12]

Even though Nixon was defeated by Democrat John F. Kennedy, Al saw huge gains in Oklahoma County. Nixon carried the county, which was heavily Democratic by registration, by more than 38,000 votes. Two Republican legislators, G.T. Blankenship and J. Thomas Taggart, were elected in Oklahoma

The Republican headquarters in Oklahoma County during the 1960 election. Al is in the background looking over canvassing charts on the wall. It was tradition to close the headquarters after the election, a tradition changed by Al when he decided to keep the GOP headquarters open year round. It became the first permanent county headquarters in Oklahoma Republican history.

County races, the first Republicans elected to the legislature from Oklahoma County since 1928. Blankenship would later become Oklahoma's only Republican attorney general in history.[13]

After the election, Al received a personal note from Vice President Nixon thanking him for his efforts and encouraging him to go the extra mile in strengthening the GOP in Oklahoma.

Republican gains gave Al the sincere belief that strong Democratic areas of Oklahoma County could be swayed to the Republican side of the political fence with the right candidates and conservative policies. In fact, Nixon's great showing in Oklahoma County prompted so many calls to the county GOP headquarters, Al kept the office open after the election to facilitate re-registration of former Democrats, meet with disgruntled voters, and process incoming telephone calls from voters who wanted to know what they could do. They believed Kennedy had stolen the election.

Al shocked party activists when he called a meeting of Oklahoma County Republicans two nights after the 1960 general election. The *Tulsa Tribune* said, "Instead of folding up his political tent and crawling away after the Nixon defeat, he called a meeting of the county Republican committee…Not only did committee members show up, but precinct and block workers were on hand, as well as Oklahoma City business leaders such as

ABOVE: The Snipes family taking a break during family weekend at YMCA Camp Classen in 1961. Front row, left to right, Marshall, Becky, and Bill. Back row, Al, Margaret Hardin, Rebecca's sister, and Rebecca.

RIGHT: The Oklahoma Republican leadership in 1960. Left to right, Phyllisjean Morris, Oklahoma County GOP vice chairman; Al, Oklahoma County Republican chairman; Julia Maddox; a representative of the Republican National Committee; Dorcas Kelly, Republican National Committeewoman from Oklahoma; and Henry Bellmon, Oklahoma Republican chairman.

John Kirkpatrick and Frank Hightower. Before the meeting was over, it had taken on the appearance of a victory party."[14]

Drew Mason, later Governor Henry Bellmon's chief of staff, was at the meeting, and recalled, "The fact that Oklahoma would elect back-to-back Republican governors in 1962 and 1966 can trace its lineage to that meeting. Al's leadership and determination came when it was needed most."[15]

Al told those gathered that much work had to be done to convince Democrats to change their party affiliation. He said, "If Andrew Jackson was alive today, he would not be in the Democrat Party!" Al rebuffed reporters' attempts to give him all the credit for GOP advances. He said, "I am just one of the people who believes in a cause and believes strong enough to fight for it—and that cause is our country!"[16]

There was no doubt that the results of the 1960 election foretold huge Republican gains in Oklahoma's future.

Al delivers $1-a-day payments to
Democratic members of the State
Senate in 1961. Accepting the check
is George Smith, left, controller of
the State Senate. *Courtesy Oklahoma
Publishing Company.*

SEVEN

Building a Two-Party System

Al Snipes is one of the true fathers of the modern Republican Party in Oklahoma.

—Lieutenant Governor Mary Fallin

WHEN REPUBLICANS CAST A SMALL SHADOW on the Oklahoma political landscape, there was little room for division or factionalism within the party. But as new GOP conservatives crept into leadership of the party, divisions arose. There was an honest disagreement as to what the philosophical foundation of the party policy should be.

Al, the consummate conservative, had a friendly but certain power struggle with Henry Bellmon who became state Republican chairman in 1960. The two men had much in common—they built their success on hard work and honesty. However, the two Republicans differed on several matters. Al was conservative in both fiscal affairs and the role of government in every day life. Bellmon was considered to be more moderate in his approach to governing because, to get things done, he had to deal with a Democrat-controlled state legislature.[1]

Bellmon remembered, "Al was more powerful than any state chairman because Oklahoma City was emerging as a Republican stronghold. There was no doubt Al was becoming a power in the state party."[2] Bellmon and Al, leaders of their respective factions in the party, disagreed on how Republican candidates should be groomed. Should a promising candidate run for election on his own personality or should he or she identify with the party to strengthen the entire ticket? Al believed every race was different. In some legislative and local races, personality of the candidate should be at the forefront. In other races, it was important to tie a candidate to the party, especially if the candidate was not well known.[3]

Bellmon and Al were different in another respect. Bellmon was out front in a leadership role as state GOP chairman while Al was the kingpin of grassroots organization. Behind the scenes, Al was developing an organization in the state's most populous county.

Even with their differences, Al had great respect for Bellmon. Al said, "As state chairman, he did more for the party than anyone has ever done. He used to come in from the farm after working all day and stay up half the night doing party work and then occasionally, he would sleep on an old couch at state headquarters to save the party money."[4] "Bellmon worked extremely hard for the party," Al said.[5]

Both Bellmon and Al focused on voter registration. It was a long standing custom in Oklahoma to register Democratic even if one identified with the Republican philosophy. The reason—most competitive races at the state and local level were decided in the Democratic primary. For most of state history before 1960, a registered Republican never got to decide major races.

Al knew that many people voted for individual candidates, but that registration was important in secondary races in which voters tended to vote for their party nominee if they were unfamiliar with the candidates.

Al realized that just registering voters would not allow the GOP to scale the hill —changes had to be made in the registration process. Democrats controlled that process with a registrar in each precinct who always encouraged new voters to register Democratic, using the age-old reason that only Democrats would have a voice in many hotly contested primaries. Al himself had fallen victim to the suggestion of a registrar. In 1946 he registered as a Democrat so he could vote in the primary for a friend of his brother-in-law. By 1948, Al had changed his registration back to Republican.

Beginning after the 1960 election, Al pushed to legalize "roving registrars," people who were licensed to register voters anywhere in the state, not just in the precinct where they lived. Al believed roving registrars could increase the number of voters switching from Democrat to Republican and would also give the rank and file something to do since they were so motivated at the time. Warren Morris, the Republican member of the Oklahoma County Election Board, and husband of Phyllisjean, the Oklahoma County GOP vice chairman, convinced board secretary H.S. "Tex" Newman that roving registrars should be expanded to include Republicans.

When Al showed up at a meeting at the election board with more than 60 people who wanted to be appointed roving registrars, the board changed its mind and denied the appointments. Al borrowed a telephone at the election board office and called *The Daily Oklahoman,* WKY-TV, and the Associated Press with his complaint that the election board would allow great latitude to the appointment of registrars for the Democratic Party and labor unions, but not for the Republicans.

The county election board convened behind closed doors and purportedly called Governor J. Howard Edmondson. When the board returned to open meeting, Al and Democrat board member W.A. "Bill" Wilson argued openly about the fairness of the process. Al ultimately won the fight and 48 Republican roving registrars were appointed later that day. It was a significant moment in the fight to make Oklahoma a two-party state.

The unprecedented organization was built door-to-door, one vote at a time. Al remembered, "The opportunity was there. Nixon losing in 1960 was a big motivating factor and people were willing to work. We realized all we had to do was to work hard and take advantage of the situation. That was the reason so many people were willing to change parties."[6]

Al's leadership efforts in changing registration of voters received a lot of publicity. Every few weeks, there were headlines such as "County GOP to Push Drive for Converts," "Republicans See 'Good Results' from House-to-House Canvass," and "County GOP to Seek Recruits."

Al, the effervescent promoter, with the help of Phyllisjean Morris, created news events. When the number of voters who switched from Democrat to Republican in Oklahoma County had topped 3,000, he and the county Republican committee hosted an old fashioned political rally and picnic to welcome the converts.

Al even received publicity when the Democrats made the news. When conservative Democrats lost their fight to modernize the party structure at the 1961 Oklahoma County Democratic Convention, Al wrote a letter to the editor of the *Oklahoma City Times:*

> The recent convention clearly indicates that there is no room in the Democratic Party for the reform of a Jeffersonian Democrat. The professionals are back in control...They are men who do not believe in constitutional reforms; men who believe our courts are a place for political favors instead of a place for justice; men who do not believe in enforcing the laws of our state unless first being exposed by the press building public sentiment to a point where they are forced to. They are men who try to cover up the lack of law enforcement by making new laws filled with loopholes, so they can go back home and defend their political buddies and other crooks the press had exposed.
>
> There isn't anything that will clean up the corrupt one party-system except a strong two-party system. There is nothing the communists would rather see than a one-party system in America, especially if it is the Democratic Party, which leans more toward socialism...Yes, you can have a hand in stopping the threat by going to the county courthouse and changing your registration to the Republican Party.[7]

In 1961 Bellmon began thinking about running for governor the following year. Oklahoma had never had a Republican governor and the state legislature had been controlled by Democrats except for one session in the state's first half-century. Bellmon knew he needed Al's help in Oklahoma County.

Republican county officials, Phyllisjean Morris, left, and Al, center, deliver a list of GOP precinct judges to Oklahoma County Election Board Secretary John L. Smith in April, 1961. *Courtesy Oklahoma Publishing Company.*

Bellmon wrote Al, "The work which you have done for the Republican Party in Oklahoma County is one of the outstanding jobs in the state, and you certainly deserve all the credit which can possibly be accorded you. Let's keep up the good work and maybe we can pat each other on the back after the inaugural in 1963."[8]

Bellmon moved the party finance office from Tulsa to Oklahoma City, a move that irritated Tulsa Republicans who had long held the scepter of GOP power in Oklahoma. The move actually brought Bellmon and Al into a closer working relationship. When the two worked into the night strategizing the growth of the Republican Party in Oklahoma, the wives, Shirley Bellmon and Rebecca Snipes, visited and went shopping together.[9] "We worked very closely together,

Al was reelected Oklahoma County GOP chairman in 1961. His influence in Republican politics was growing each year. *Courtesy Oklahoma Publishing Company.*

did a lot together—it was a lot of effort," Bellmon remembered.[10]

At the 1961 Oklahoma County GOP convention, Al was reelected chairman without opposition and Marilyn Harris was elected vice chairman to replace Phyllisjean Morris, who had become vice chairman of the state party structure. Al told delegates they still had a lot of work to do. In 1961, voter registration in Oklahoma showed 940,702 Democrats and only 215,344 Republicans. If Republicans had any chance of winning the governor's race in 1962, there was much work to be done.

Oklahoma County Republicans also voted to support right-to-work legislation and legislative reapportionment to force the legislature to redraw State Senate and House of Representative district lines to reflect the population that was moving from rural to urban Oklahoma. Interestingly, the right-to-work issue, that supported legislation to prohibit unions from requiring everyone working in a unionized company to become a member of the union, stewed on the back burner of Oklahoma politics for another four decades. In 2000, voters passed a right-to-work law in Oklahoma, with the help of Al's son, Marshall, who served as state treasurer of the group supporting passage of the act. The seeds planted by Al and his Republican compatriots such as Bill Boulton in 1961 sprouted over the decades and bloomed fully into success in 2000.

Al's stand on right-to-work and GOP inroads into Democratic strongholds in Oklahoma City brought him into the gun sights of J.D. McCarty, a south Oklahoma City Democrat who had risen to become Speaker of the Oklahoma House of Representatives. McCarty, who wielded significant power at the State Capitol, vigorously opposed right-to-work. Every time Al appeared at a local civic club, womens' group, or chamber of commerce meeting with his message about right-to-work, McCarty followed with his allegations that passage of a right-to-work law prohibiting compulsory unionism would effectively destroy collective bargaining in Oklahoma.[11]

Oklahoma Republicans were gaining national prominence. In January, 1962, the Republican National Committee held a meeting in Oklahoma City. Al, Bellmon, and many others worked hard to host the nation's top Republicans.[12] Al was ably assisted by Mickey Edwards, president of the Oklahoma Young Republicans, who was later elected to Congress from Oklahoma's Fifth District in a campaign managed by Al's son, Marshall. Edwards served 16 years in Congress. The Republican National Committee meeting in Oklahoma was without incident. Bellmon remembered, "It came off without a hitch."[13]

Al fought Democrats on several fronts, including the question of federal aid to education. Al believed that once local school districts depended upon federal money, it would not be long until the federal government ruled education. It was only a matter of time until circumstances proved that Al and many others who opposed federal aid to education were correct in their theory.

Grace Boulton joined forces with Al on the federal aid to education issue. She was involved in the parent teacher organization at Grover Cleveland Elementary School and could not believe that local educators would allow the federal government to dictate programs by giving money to local school districts. Al and Boulton attended the state Parent Teachers Association meeting at Enid and convinced delegates, over the strong objection of the teachers' lobby, to oppose federal aid to education.[14]

In February, 1962, Bellmon officially resigned as chairman of the Oklahoma Republican Party and announced his candidacy for governor. Because of deep strife within the Oklahoma

Democratic Party and national conservative trends, Oklahoma Republicans smelled blood. One newspaper commentary said, "If out of the infighting of the Democratic primaries there emerges a candidate who does not suit the temper of the Oklahoma voters, they might turn in their disappointment to Bellmon. This is the way it has happened in other one-party states when the minority party was able to slip into power after the brawling factions of the majority party had knocked each other out."[15]

The Oklahoma GOP fielded a formidable statewide slate of candidates in 1962, headed by Bellmon as the gubernatorial candidate and B. Hayden Crawford, the former United States Attorney in Tulsa, who was trying to unseat longtime United States Senator A.S. "Mike" Monroney. Crawford had given Senator Robert S. Kerr a scare in 1960, largely due to the Nixon 160,000-vote margin in Oklahoma.

Al, the master publicity-getter, took advantage of the opportunity to draw attention to what he believed was irresponsible behavior by the Democrat-controlled legislature. He came up with a unique idea while legislators were still in session in the spring of 1962. Al believed that almost anything the State Senate passed was bad for Oklahoma and was designed to continue the "Old Guard" domination by Democrats.

Al convinced the executive committee of the Oklahoma County Republican Party to authorize $1-a-day-payments to Democratic state senators while they remained in session. Al believed that if the State Senate could remain in session all year, past the general election, their actions would further alienate Oklahoma voters. A photograph of Al handing the checks for senators to the Senate controller was big news in local newspapers. Senator Everett Collins, president pro tempore of the State Senate, later returned the checks to the GOP county committee.

Al's ploy drew fire from Woody Hunt, Oklahoma County Democratic Chairman, who said, "It seems like instead of coming up with a constructive program, they're acting like a bunch of playboys with more money than they know what to do with." Hunt still was stinging from reports that his picture was prominently displayed on a dart board at the Oklahoma County Republican headquarters.[16]

The bloodbath that Democratic leaders feared in the 1962 primary unfolded before the voters of the state. After a hard-fought Democratic primary that featured big names such as Lieutenant Governor George Nigh, George Miskovsky, Preston Moore, and State Senator Fred Harris, former Governor Raymond Gary and Midwest City builder W.P. "Bill" Atkinson slugged it out in a runoff that deeply divided Oklahoma Democrats.

In a runoff election that shocked the most veteran political analysts, Gary, who had a large lead in the primary, lost to Atkinson by only 449 votes, out of nearly a half million votes cast. A one vote change in less than one fourth of the state's precincts would have changed the outcome of the election.[17]

As a result of the quarrel among Democrats, the Herculean effort of Al and other Republican leaders to change thousands of Democrats into registered Republicans, the front-page opposition of *The Daily Oklahoman* to Atkinson, and the early signs of Oklahoma Democrats leaving the more liberal tendencies of the national Democratic Party, Bellmon was elected as Oklahoma's first Republican governor. Atkinson was so incensed about *The Daily Oklahoman's* involvement in the election, he founded his own newspaper, *The Oklahoma Journal.*

Oklahoma had taken the first step to becoming a two-party state—and Al had the last laugh on his pastor at Capitol Hill Baptist Church. The week before the election, Reverend Hugh

R. Bumpass, who had officiated at Al and Rebecca's wedding 15 years before and had baptized their children, announced that the next governor of Oklahoma would be in the pulpit the next Sunday. Reverend Bumpass apparently believed Atkinson would be elected and had lined him up to speak. Al was disappointed. When Atkinson lost, the pastor was in a quandary. In a panic, he called Al and asked if he could invite Bellmon to church on Sunday. Al happily declined.

The All-American Snipes family in
1963. Left to right, Al, Bill, Becky,
Marshall, and Rebecca.

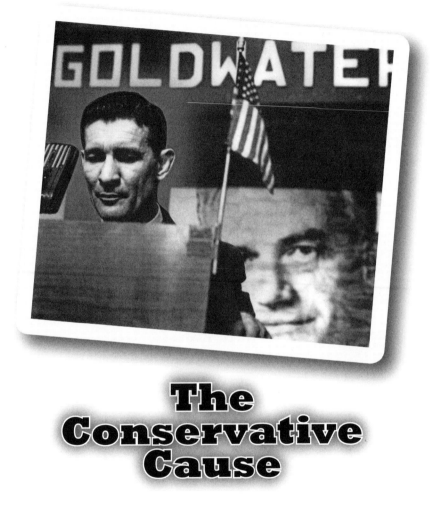

EIGHT

The Conservative Cause

The conservative approach is nothing more or less than an attempt to apply the wisdom and experience and the revealed truths of the past to the problems of today.

—Barry Goldwater

AL WAS THE UNOFFICIAL HEAD of the conservative wing of the Oklahoma Republican Party as Henry Bellmon took office as the first GOP governor in 1963. Even though disagreements between Bellmon and Al were well known to party faithful, both men got along and worked for the growth of the Republican movement. Bellmon appointed Al as vice chairman of his Inaugural Parade Committee and Al was in charge of distributing tickets in Oklahoma County to the events surrounding Bellmon's inauguration on January 14, 1963.

It was no secret that Bellmon's supporters would prefer to replace Al as Oklahoma County Republican chairman. Otis Sullivant, the veteran political writer for *The Daily Oklahoman*, wrote openly about Bellmon forces wanting to replace Al.

Shortly after Henry Bellmon became the state's first GOP governor in 1963, the Oklahoma County Republican leadership was invited to the governor's office. Al sits in the governor's chair. Left to right, standing, are Dr. J. Raymond Stacy, Don Kinkaid, Bellmon, an unidentified worker, G.T. Blankenship, Marilyn Harris, and Tom Harris.

But Sullivant surmised, "In fact, those county Republicans who want to defeat Snipes, if he runs again, haven't been able to get a candidate of sufficient strength to take on Snipes."[1]

Al perceived that Bellmon changed his attitude toward the Republican Party structure once he was elected governor. One of the first problems was that Bellmon, as governor, wanted to pick the new state chairman. Al and other activists disagreed. Al was opposed to the idea because he believed the grassroots Republicans should elect their leaders, rather than having an elected official hand pick the head of the party.[2]

Despite opposition from Bellmon supporters, Al and Marilyn Harris were reelected as chairman and vice chairman of the Oklahoma County Republicans in 1963. However, Al's position did not fare as well at the Republican State Convention held at Oklahoma City's Municipal Auditorium. Forrest Beall had succeeded Bellmon as state Republican chairman and was running for reelection. Al supported Thomas J. Harris, the husband of Oklahoma County GOP vice chairman, Marilyn Harris. Bellmon backed a third candidate, State Representative William R. "Bill" Burkett. The three-way battle pointed toward a free-for-all on the convention floor. There was also talk that B. Hayden Crawford, who had campaigned for the United States Senate as a right-wing Republican, might take the state chairmanship if drafted, although Crawford told reporters he was not an active candidate for the job.[3]

Before the convention, Bellmon broke his silence and publicly announced his support for Burkett, effectively dumping the reelection effort by Beall. Al took exception to Bellmon, as governor, trying to influence the selection of the chair of the state party. However, he was pleased that Bellmon was rejecting the reelection of Beall. Al also thought Burkett to be a very capable and dedicated Republican leader.

Al took the lead in pushing Crawford to accept the job. "We will nominate him," Al told a reporter, after talking to Crawford for 40 minutes on the telephone. Al and Don D. Kinkaid, who had introduced a resolution at the Oklahoma County convention to bind their state convention votes for Crawford, predicted Crawford would accept the chairmanship if a majority of the convention delegates favored him. After Crawford dropped out of the race, Al was instrumental in convincing Harris to enter.[4]

Young Republicans also opposed Bellmon's handpicking of Burkett as state chairman. Mickey Edwards, chairman of the Oklahoma Young Republican Federation, said, "We believe that Governor Bellmon has now backed out of an earlier pledge to remain neutral in this contest."[5]

Governor Bellmon's wishes prevailed and Burkett was elected state Republican chairman. Political writer Otis Sullivant summarized Bellmon's actions:

> Governor Bellmon faces a task of healing the bruises and wounded feelings left by his forcing the state Republicans convention to select...Burkett as chairman. Bellmon is mistaken if he thinks the battle left no "sore spots." Bellmon said there will be no punishment of those who opposed him.

> It was no smashing victory for Bellmon...Burkett beat Beall 598 to 557 after Harris had been eliminated in the first vote. Bellmon went farther than any Oklahoma governor to elect a party chairman.

Bellmon was about as gentle and subtle as a freight train. He had declared he wouldn't participate, appeared to favor Beall quietly, then declared for Burkett. He tried to get the candidates to reach an agreement, said he would not put pressure on delegates, then came to the convention and threw the full force of the administration in it."[6]

Other observers noticed that Oklahoma and Tulsa County Republicans were hesitant to follow the governor's lead. Many party members believed Bellmon had overreached himself. In the final analysis, the fighting for leadership of the party was a sign of the virility of the new Oklahoma Republican Party. One writer said, "But all concerned must be careful that what starts out as a healthy intra-party competition doesn't slide into bitter bickering that tears an organization apart."[7]

Bellmon recalled, "My concern was that Tom Harris, leader of the party's right wing faction, would beat Forrest Beall who, unlike, Tom Harris, was not a very dynamic speaker. I could not support Beall if he was going to lose and I sure did not want Harris elected to take the party way out to the right. So, I asked Bill Burkett to run."[8]

Burkett and Beall won the first battle to eliminate Harris. Burkett wanted to drop out and allow Beall to be elected. But Bellmon was against that maneuver—it would have been seen as a defeat for the newly elected governor. Recognizing the gravity of the decision, Al, Harris, and others ultimately supported Burkett.[9]

The Republicans were not alone in dissension within the ranks. Al took advantage of growing splits within the Democratic Party. Defeated gubernatorial candidate Bill Atkinson called Democrats who voted for Bellmon "turncoats" and called for the ouster of any Democratic county official who supported Bellmon in the governor's race. On the heels of Atkinson's blast, Al accused Atkinson and other Democratic leaders of showing "real dictator desires." Al said, "Threatening to punish those within their party who do not work and vote the straight party ticket…is a brazen exercise of power on their part…If you disagree with Democrat leaders, you put yourself in a class of undesirables."[10]

Mickey Edwards, later elected to the United States House of Representatives from Oklahoma's fifth congressional district, was 24 years old when he met Al. Edwards, assistant city editor of the *Oklahoma City Times,* wanted to be involved in Republican politics, so he contacted Al. Edwards remembered, "The day I met Al, he put me to work. It was not a small job—he put me in a big job, working at the precinct level."[11]

Edwards and Al both agreed on one thing—the GOP in Oklahoma was an embattled minority, almost a non-existent minority when Al began organizing Republicans at the grassroots level. Edwards quickly recognized that Al was a master of organization and recruiting good GOP candidates. Edwards said, "Al mastered the art of recruiting candidates—that's how you build an organization. Al knew the philosophy of organizing people as well as anyone in any company, anywhere."[12]

One of the landmark battles in the fight over control of the Oklahoma legislature occurred in 1963 when litigation involving the reapportionment of the legislature reached the federal courts. Shortly after the United States Supreme Court declared that apportionment must be based upon the one-person-one-vote theory, a special panel of three federal judges, Alfred P. Murrah, Ross Rizley, and Fred Daugherty, held Oklahoma's legislative apportionment unconstitutional.

The battle then shifted to what remedy would be chosen to correct the situation. The state's largest cities benefited greatly from the federal court decision that clearly stated that Oklahoma's legislature would never reapportion itself on its own. There was too much at stake—a long battle between rural and urban forces. It was the first time a federal court had issued such a sweeping decree to intervene in the political affairs of a state.

Even though the federal court has issued a decisive win for citizens of metropolitan counties, Al branded the decision a "halfway" job. Al said the court was wrong in giving the legislature one more chance to reapportion itself. In the end, Al was right. The legislature's attempts were inadequate and the courts later invalidated the results of the 1964 primaries.

In an effort to quickly fix the problem, the federal court entrusted the job to Patience Latting, a Phi Beta Kappa graduate of the University of Oklahoma and holder of a master's degree in mathematics and statistics from Columbia University. Al secretly gave his suggested map of the Oklahoma County district lines to Latting who worked from her kitchen table to redistrict the entire state. Al could not publicly announce his choice of district lines, because his support would doom the information, at least in some circles. Eventually, Al's plan for Oklahoma County was approved with only minor changes.[13]

Latting, who later served on the city council and as mayor of Oklahoma City, the first woman mayor in a United States city exceeding 200,000 in population, produced a redistricting plan that was approved by the federal court and changed forever the makeup of the two houses of the Oklahoma legislature and brought major changes in the state's political culture. Latting later appointed Al to the citizens advisory committee to the South Canadian River Basin project. Al was elected chairman of the group.

It is easy to summarize Al's involvement in Arizona United States Senator Barry Goldwater's campaign for the presidency

Al rides an elephant in an Oklahoma City parade in 1964 to publicize the candidacy of presidential nominee Barry Goldwater and United States Senate candidate Bud Wilkinson.

in 1964. Al and others in Oklahoma were the first delegates to officially commit their votes to be cast at the 1964 Republican National Convention. It was not an easy road and split further the already frayed elements of the Oklahoma Republican Party. Governor Bellmon was accused of not enthusiastically support- ing the conservative Goldwater. Bellmon remembered, "I was for Goldwater, but I was under suspicion—no one believed me! I was never accepted as a member of the inner circle among Goldwater supporters."14

State Senator Denzil Garrison, state chairman of the Goldwater campaign and vice chairman of the Oklahoma delegation, recalled, "Bellmon was for Goldwater. I remember him saying that Oklahoma was the first state to 'marry Barry.'"15

Oklahoma Republicans massed their support behind Goldwater. After the Oklahoma County Republican convention, one newspaper headline screamed, "It's Barry Day at GOP Parley." The *Oklahoma City Times* reported, "With the fervor of tent revivalists, Republicans of the fifth congressional district prepared Saturday to jump aboard the Barry Goldwater bandwagon."16

Al and Thomas J. Harris were elected as the fifth district's delegates to the national convention in San Francisco, California. When Al was nominated as a delegate, he was given credit for building the Republican Party in Oklahoma County to "unprecedented strength."

Al was excited about attending the national convention in San Francisco, even though the Oklahoma delegation was anything but cohesive in its support for Goldwater who easily won the presidential nomination. Al was a floor leader for the Midwest region for Goldwater along with State Senator Denzil Garrison.

As floor leaders, Al and Garrison sat next to each other on the convention floor. Directly behind the Oklahoma delegation sat the Pennsylvania delegation. Behind Al and Garrison sat Pennsylvania Governor Raymond P. Shafer who was running the floor campaign of Nelson Rockefeller, Goldwater's opponent. Shafer's every decision was relayed by telephone to Clifton White, Goldwater's campaign manager. When Governor Shafer discovered what was happening, he made other communications arrangements.17

Al wore a huge campaign button that said, "STAMP OUT HUNTLEY BRINKLEY," a reference to NBC news anchors

Chet Huntley and David Brinkley. Most Republicans, including Al, believed that Huntley and Brinkley slanted the national news toward a liberal Democratic Party view. Seeing that slant as a negative influence on Republican ideas and candidates, Al proudly wore the button.

It was the day of political campaigns being televised gavel to gavel. When one of the cameras recorded Al wearing his Huntley-Brinkley button, Brinkley sought out Al on the convention floor and challenged Al to explain the button and its negative tone. Al replied, "I would be happy to answer your questions, but only on live national television." Brinkley told Al he would go get a camera crew and return shortly. Brinkley never returned. Al always maintained that Brinkley knew the answer and did not want Al to be heard as a spokesman for the conservative viewpoint.[18]

Al was disappointed when Goldwater was defeated soundly both nationally and in Oklahoma by incumbent President Lyndon B. Johnson, from the neighboring state of Texas. Another casualty of the Johnson landslide in Oklahoma was the United States Senate candidacy of former University of Oklahoma football coach Charles "Bud" Wilkinson by State Senator Fred Harris, a Democrat. Wilkinson's entry into the race provided the fodder for another political battle between Al's conservative wing and Bellmon's moderate wing of the Oklahoma Republican Party.

Al initially supported Thomas J. Harris, the vice president and general manager of Aero Commander, who was described by political pundits as "ultraconservative" for the nomination. Al was concerned that Wilkinson, even though he was a respected football coach and had a popular name, was not loyal enough to the party structure. In fact, Wilkinson's campaign was run separately from the Goldwater campaign in Oklahoma in 1964.

The button worn by Al and other Republican activists at the 1964 Republican National Convention as a protest to what the GOP considered the newscasters' left slant to the news.

After the Wilkinson defeat, Drew Mason, Governor Bellmon's administrative assistant, blamed the Oklahoma County Republicans, particularly Al, for not supporting Wilkinson as much as they supported Goldwater's candidacy.[19]

In truth, what allowed Democrat Fred Harris to beat the popular Wilkinson, was the massive vote totals rolled up by President Johnson. Harris no doubt rode Johnson's coattails into the United States Senate.

Despite the Democratic landslide, Republicans made gains in Oklahoma County, with eight victories. Elected to the State Senate were Dr. Richard Stansberry and Ted Findeiss. Republican House of Representatives members re-elected were G.T. Blankenship and J. Thomas Taggart. Also elected to the Oklahoma House were George Camp, Bill Holaday, and Dr. John W. Drake. J.P. "Dick" Richardson was elected the first Republican county commissioner in Oklahoma County in history. Despite the Johnson landslide, never had so many Republicans been elected in any county in Oklahoma history.

Never a quitter, Al took the losses of the 1964 election in stride and moved on, looking for new Republican candidates and intensified his effort to change the face of Oklahoma County from Democrat to Republican.

NINE

The Kingmaker

Oklahoma's Republican Party has a new chairman.
It also has a new and controversial kingmaker.

—*AMARILLO DAILY NEWS*

A L WAS NOT BASHFUL ABOUT ASKING PEOPLE to give money to support Republican candidates and causes. He believed that one should contribute to the political party of his choice because, by doing so, he is buying a share in good government. Al said, "by small individual contributions to a political party, you are assured of adequate campaign financing, thereby precluding the need for large gifts from pressure and vested-interest groups."[1]

Al disputed detractors of the party structure who considered contributions to the Republican Party inappropriate. Al said, "Why should it come as a surprise that it takes money to operate a political organization? In all our outside-of-family activities, we take it for granted that money is required. We give to our church, civic clubs, Boy Scouts, schools, and a host of other special activities, all serving worthy purposes." "Give to your political party," Al said, "and know it is your free expression and opportunity to support your choice of government."[2]

Most special interest money went to Democratic candidates because they were in control of government. Accordingly, all Republican money came from individuals who simply wanted good government. Al remembered, "The odds were stacked heavily against us."[3] Vernon Bealls, Thomas J. Harris, and C. Hubert Gragg were the fundraisers for the party and were indispensable assets to the GOP.

Al's no-holds-barred support for Goldwater in the 1964 presidential election and his conservative beliefs continued to draw criticism and opposition from some ranks. Al resisted efforts by Governor Bellmon and some of his aides to influence the selection of chairmen of county Republican organizations.

A sore spot between Al and other county chairmen and Bellmon's office involved the governor's appointments to boards and commissions and hiring for state jobs. Al charged that Bellmon's staff did not consult the party before making appointments. Al was upset that state engineering contracts went to a Republican architect "who never designed a road in his life," and, in his opinion, an "incompetent Republican" was named to head the State Planning and Resources Board.[4]

"It was an impossible task." Bellmon recalled, "Involvement of the county chairman complicated the process because we were required to get the local senator of each appointment to agree to move confirmation through the State Senate, or appointments would never happen.[5] Because there were only four GOP senators, the governor's appointment process was very difficult.

Al was unhappy over Bellmon not agreeing to his suggestion that Jim Wade, an executive of Aero Commander, be appointed to the Aeronautical Board. Al complained to the governor about the appointment of the pilot of a Democrat to the commission.[6]

When a slot came open for a state board or commission appointment in Oklahoma County, Al requested that the governor's office obtain the county party's input. But time and time again, the party's input was ignored. Drew Mason, Bellmon's administrative assistant in charge of appointments, was quick to respond to Al's criticism of the governor for not appointing a Republican replacement for Oklahoma Supreme Court Justice Earl Welch who had been indicted for federal income tax evasion. Before Bellmon appointed District Judge Ralph B. Hodges, Democrat from Durant, Oklahoma, Mason said, "There just aren't enough Republicans to fill the appointments. That's really the reason Al hates me."[7]

Drew Mason vividly recalls how upset Al was when he failed to consult him about gubernatorial appointments. Mason said, "No matter how hard we tried to accommodate the party, we

Governor Bellmon's administrative assistant, Drew Mason, and Al were often at odds on how the Republican Party should operate in Oklahoma. In later years, they became friends and had a deep mutual respect for each other's ideas. *Courtesy Oklahoma Publishing Company.*

could not manage to get past the State Senate with which the process forced us to deal."[8]

There was no doubt that Al's building of a strong and powerful Oklahoma County Republican Party ruffled feathers. Al's fighting spirit and leftover hard feelings from the Wilkinson defeat in 1964 created pockets of resistance and a sure and certain "anti-Snipes" faction that operated in both the county and state GOP organizations. It was obvious that Al was not reappointed to the State Republican Executive Committee to maintain the state group as a Bellmon machine. It had been customary to appoint the Oklahoma and Tulsa County chairmen to the state executive committee.[9]

Mary Lu Tracewell Gordon, in her graduate thesis at the University of Oklahoma, summarized the squabble between Al and his opponents:

> Until Al Snipes became county chairman, the Oklahoma County Republican Party had been run like an auxiliary of the Junior League. He made a political party out of it and there is resentment from the old leaders—the "silk stocking" set.
>
> Oklahoma County Republicans today seem to fall into two categories, those who are for Al Snipes and those who are against him. Those who are against him are a combination of pro-Bellmon Republicans, liberal Republicans, and ultra-conservative Republicans. But Snipes has managed to keep tight control on the party organization in the county and through this control he has established Oklahoma County as a powerful influence in the state party.[10]

Until 1965, Al had never drawn an opponent in his election as county Republican chairman. But that year, there was a move to replace him. The Village Mayor Wesley Mowery made a strong move to oust Al as county chairman. Newspaper reporters recognized the attempts of Bellmon supporters to defeat Al and remove his voice, a sure thorn in the side of the state GOP party. One reporter wrote, "A move is underway among

Oklahoma County Republicans for new leadership to replace Al Snipes, insurance man, as county chairman. It will involve a test of whether capital county Republicans want to move away from the ultra conservatism of Senator Barry Goldwater to a more moderate stand for the future."[11]

There was fighting at every corner of the 1965 Republican convention in Oklahoma County. As at the convention the year before, approximately 1,000 people attended, both record turnouts that never have been equaled. There was an early battle over who would be named temporary chairman to gavel the opening of the convention. Mowery, the mayor of The Village, selected State Representative G.T. Blankenship to serve as temporary chairman, while Al favored attorney Carmon C. Harris to fill the slot. Al was surprised by a public announcement that Blankenship wanted to be temporary chairman because Harris had been already unanimously selected by the county party's executive committee. In the end, Blankenship, minority leader of the Oklahoma House of Representatives, dropped his candidacy.[12]

Mowery claimed victory before the February 13 convention. He told Otis Sullivant, political writer for *The Daily Oklahoman,* "From all the arm twisting, I think they [Snipes supporters] are using figures for a smoke screen. I think they are in trouble and we are going to win."[13]

Al was calm in his approach to be reelected as county chairman. His response was, "I am not campaigning. I have served the party a long time. If the people want me again, I will serve. I don't intend to make one phone call or spend a penny. If my record of service was good enough to justify my running again, I suppose they will elect me. If not, I suppose they will find someone with a better record and elect him."[14]

Al had to recant on his promise not to campaign in his bid for a fourth term as county chairman because of what he labeled "lies" being told about him. Al said he would not sit idly by and be persecuted with falsehoods. As a direct slap at what he perceived Governor Bellmon's office was doing in trying to influence the outcome of the chairman's election, Al offered to drop out of the race if Bellmon would fire administrative assistant Drew Mason. Al charged that Mason was pressuring various people, including the county GOP

Al talks strategy with Gladys Gockel, center, and Jewel Matthews during the 1965 Oklahoma County GOP Convention. Matthews was secretary of the Oklahoma County Republican Party and longtime ally of Al. She kept the headquarters organized and coordinated. She was a tremendous asset to the party and she and her husband, Bob, became close friends of Al and Rebecca. *Courtesy Oklahoma Publishing Company.*

legislative delegation, to oppose Al. Bellmon did not accept
Al's offer.[15]

In addition to the chairman's race at the convention, there
was a hotly contested vice-chairman's race between Mrs. James
B. Eskridge, III, and Gladys Gockel, who also served as Al's
campaign manager. There was no doubt that all issues in the
county convention would hinge on how many precinct workers
Al and his supporters could bring to the meeting.

Again, Al's superior organizational ability brought him a
resounding victory at the county convention—but it came after
floor fights over credentials, the use of voice votes, and approval
of the unit-rule for use at the state GOP convention later that
month. Al somehow won the fight to, in effect, allow the
majority of the delegates in Oklahoma County to determine
how the county's 239 votes on the second ballot would be cast
at the state convention under the unit rule.[16]

One of the main areas of controversy at the county convention was the use of voice votes. It was pointed out that delegates
with fractional votes sounded as loud as delegates with full
votes—and that a fair assessment of their votes was impossible.
The Mowery forces claimed they were out-screamed, not out-
voted, after a voice vote was used to pass several controversial
resolutions on the floor. However, the official records of the
convention show that many more delegates were present from
pro-Al sections of the county than from areas where delegates
tended to oppose Al.[17]

Al's reelection came on a voice vote. A motion that his elec-
tion be made unanimous passed, but had noisy opposition.
Also reelected was Gladys Gockel as county vice chairman.
Al never knew any party worker who put in more volunteer
time and effort than Gockel who later received the first Al
Snipes Lifetime Achievement Award from the Metro Young

Republicans. Dr. Ray Stacy was elected state committeeman and Grace Boulton was elected state committeewoman.

The Daily Oklahoman called Al's reelection "a defeat of Governor Henry Bellmon and the county GOP legislative delegations." A newspaper story said, "Bellmon and Snipes have had their differences in recent years and it is known the governor would have liked to see the incumbent replaced."[18]

Letters to the editor of Oklahoma City newspapers knocked Al's leadership and his handling of the convention, alleging that Al and his forces ran roughshod over anyone attempting to express a differing opinion. However, the most powerful response was on the editorial page of the *Oklahoma City Times*:

> Any who assumed the resounding defeat of Senator Goldwater in Oklahoma as elsewhere would bring an inevitable Republican swing toward the middle got a jolt Saturday. The Oklahoma County Republican convention reelected what is in essence Goldwaterite leadership and repudiated a strong effort to make a change in a more moderate direction. Al Snipes of Oklahoma City retained his post as county chairman, turning back a threat by Wesley Mowery…The question now is what the Snipes faction will do with its victory, and whether it has learned from the Goldwater defeat of last year and will attempt to make the party more inclusive by making a more broadly-based appeal than in the past.[19]

Al believed that the newspaper editorial writers were missing the point—the underpinnings of the conservative movement were in the hearts and minds of many Americans. Later, it was the lack of compromise of beliefs and refusal to move toward the middle on fundamental issues that led to the Ronald Reagan revolution in the 1980s.[20]

Boulton's election began her 24-year stint as a GOP party leader, including a 16-year stint as national committeewoman. Al said, "She held the party's feet to the fire on the core issues of lower taxes and limited government."[21] Boulton later served in some of the most important positions in the GOP, including state vice chairman and a member of the National Platform Committee and the National Rules Committee. She and her husband, Don, became close friends with Al and Rebecca.

Even though Grace Boulton assumed major leadership roles, she believed she was part of the team. She said, "Al was persistent in getting the work done. I remember one time my mother and I were canning peaches when Al called and said he needed me to come to the election board that afternoon and copy names. He was hard to turn down because you knew he would be there too." Boulton called Al, "the head of the team."[22]

With the county convention concluded, Al's battleground moved to Tulsa, the site of the 1965 Republican State Convention. The first fight was over the unit rule, which allowed a county to vote as a unit, rather than by individual delegates, after the second ballot. In other words, the county chairman could vote, with consent of a majority of county delegates, his group as a bloc. That would allow the county to have a greater say in affairs of the state convention according to party rules. The unit rule was allowed to remain part of the party rules.

The main business of the state convention was the election of the chairman. Three candidates were at the forefront. Truman Branscum, the moderate candidate, was the choice of Governor Bellmon and outgoing state chairman Bill Burkett. Roger Rensvold, a conservative and anti-Bellmon candidate, was backed by Tom Harris, Mickey Edwards, and other die-hard conservatives. E.L. "Bud" Stewart, Jr., was a relative moderate and Al's choice as state chairman.[23] Al believed Rensvold was too far to the right and that Stewart would be a more effective leader.

On the first ballot, the Oklahoma County delegation split their votes with the most votes going for Rensvold. When Rensvold ran third in the statewide balloting, delegates were left with a runoff between Branscum and Stewart.

The race was neck and neck. All delegates waited with anticipation to see who Oklahoma County, with its 239 votes, would favor as state chairman. Because Al had prevailed in having the party's unit rule followed at the county convention, he took the microphone and announced that all 239 votes of Oklahoma County, and the chairmanship of the Oklahoma Republican Party, went to Stewart. Al had won again! Bud Stewart remembered, "Because of the unit rule, Oklahoma County had the power to sway results."[24]

Bellmon aide, Drew Mason, accused Al of playing petty politics at the expense of the party and said the Oklahoma County party organization was infested with ultra-conservative members of the John Birch Society.[25]

Al defended his record. He said there was not one member of the Birch Society in any active position in the county party organization. "I won't permit it," he said, "I don't want anyone in a position of leadership whose loyalty to a private organization is above his loyalty to the Republican Party."[26]

The facts also backed Al. Since he had become chairman, registration in Oklahoma County had dropped from six-to-one Republican, to four-to-one Republican.

One newspaper assessment of the county and state Republican conventions in 1965 said, "The rising county chairman from Capitol Hill will be a man to watch in the next couple of years." Al was beginning to be referred to as a "kingmaker."[27]

The differences between Al and Bellmon were never personal. Bellmon remembered, "I never felt anything but good will toward Al. We got along very well. He was selfless—he was not in politics for himself."[28]

Al had great respect for Bellmon. Al said, "Henry was the father of the GOP in Oklahoma—no one did more for the state in building a two-party system. He was honest, hardworking and did not back down from what he believed."

Neither Bellmon or Al ever lost respect for each other. In fact, Al worked hard for Bellmon in elections for governor and United States Senate.

RIGHT: The impeccable qualities of the Vondel Smith family helped Smith to pull off one of Oklahoma's greatest political upsets in 1966. This photograph appeared in campaign literature.

TEN

The Turning Point

The 1966 election signaled the end of a one-party system of state government in Oklahoma. The election of Dewey Bartlett as a second Republican governor and the defeat of House Speaker J.D. McCarty gave birth to two-party government in Oklahoma.

—Bob Burke

AFTER THE **1965** R**EPUBLICAN** S**TATE** C**ONVENTION,** the rumblings of division that had plagued the GOP for two years came fully into the light of day. A newspaper headline, "Sadly Divided GOP," summed up the undercurrent of infighting between conservatives and moderates, pro-Al Snipes and anti-Al Snipes factions.

The division carried over to the young Republican organizations of the county. The original county Republican group, the Oklahoma County Young Republican Club (County Young Republicans), had been taken over by pro-Al forces in 1965. Many of the club's conservative members had broken away and formed the Capitol City Republican Club. A third group, formed in early 1966 by Mickey Edwards and Julie Wherry, was the Greater Oklahoma City Young Republican Club.[1]

Many of the young Republicans who had opposed Al's reelection as county chairman organized a Republican Action Committee (RAC), as a committee of the Oklahoma County Young Republican Club. Bellmon aide Drew Mason and Ray Tompkins, chairman of the County Young Republicans, were the backbone of the new group that publicly opposed Al and the official policies of the Oklahoma County Republican Party.

The anti-Al group met twice monthly and had an impressive list of officers and advisors including Governor Bellmon, Harl Stokes, Beverly Schrader, George Massad, Margaret Eskridge, Dean Mikkelson, Ethel Nisley, John Tyler, Dorothy Stanislaus, Clyde Wheeler, and the Oklahoma County legislative delegation.[2]

However, the veiled attempt to dethrone Al never was successful. Drew Mason later said, "I think we hurt Snipes, and I think we hurt the county organization on one hand, but on the other hand we filled no need or gap. All we did was hold a big fund raising dinner which cost us about as much as we raised.

We couldn't attract people for the day-to-day precinct work. The kind of people who will do that work were working for the county party. We were nothing but a big paper tiger."[3]

State GOP Chairman Bud Stewart feared the RAC would damage the Republican effort in Oklahoma County in the upcoming 1966 election, so he called for a meeting with Al, Drew Mason, Ray Tompkins, and the Oklahoma County Executive Committee. The result was that the RAC was abolished and existing leadership in Ward Two would be allowed to continue. The leadership had been opposed to Al.[4]

The RAC controversy actually healed relations between Mason and Al. It was Al's idea to give his opponents more voice in the party. Al even offered the County Young Republicans membership on all county subcommittees and chairmanship of two of the subcommittees of the county executive committee. Mason, who Al offered to name as chairman of the County Finance Committee, said, "Al did more than anyone to heal a breach in the party organization."[5] In the decades that followed, Mason and Al developed a healthy respect for each other's work in the Republican Party.

Mason recalled, "There were many prominent members of the GOP, but it was Henry and Al who were the powers that changed the political color of Oklahoma."[6]

Another galvanizing force for the party was state chairman Bud Stewart who had not been Bellmon's first choice, but nevertheless was acceptable to the governor. Stewart was a major force in unifying the party. He said, "It was a united effort—we all wanted to elect Republicans."[7]

True to form, Al never let party politics and fighting with fellow Republicans cloud his vision of Republican supremacy in Oklahoma County. With the RAC division behind him, Al set his sights on the 1966 election. He was determined to support the Oklahoma County Republican legislators who had worked for his ouster. Al saw the big picture—Oklahoma must be a true two-party state, and 1966 was when that dream could potentially be realized. Al also supported G.T. Blankenship in his bid to be elected Oklahoma's first Republican attorney general. Al had great respect for Blankenship and worked hard in his campaign.

In the meantime, Al continued his relentless pursuit to register Republicans. At a much-publicized reregistration rally and victory party, Al announced the conversion of 133 Democrats.

Not for a moment did Al take lightly the job of converting Oklahoma to a two-party system. He realized that the Democrat ratio of registered voters was still over four-to-one in Oklahoma County, 177,040 to 41,346. Only one fourth of the Oklahoma County legislators were Republican. In the 1964 race, the Republican candidate for Congress received only 31.1 percent of the vote. Even though GOP candidates had been gobbled up by the Johnson landslide, Republicans were still optimistic about the 1966 contests.[8]

As Republicans looked past personal differences to promote GOP candidates, there was more cooperation between the state and county party. Al worked with members of the Oklahoma State GOP Executive Committee such as Bud Stewart, Dorothy Stanislaus, Governor Bellmon, G.T. Blankenship, Denzil Garrison, James Unruh, Skip Healey, and Grace Boulton.

In addition to party officials, the GOP was blessed with dedicated volunteers and county party officials such as Ash and Gladys Gockel, Blaine and Carolyn Miller, Don and Grace Boulton, Ron Wallace, Mickey Edwards, Phyllisjean and Warren Morris, Marilyn and Tom Harris, Betty Brake, Ann Taylor, Nancy Apgar, Jewell and Bob Matthews, Pat and Ann Patterson, and Tom and Kay Dudley. Gladys Gockel was county vice chairman, Phyllisjean Morris was state vice chairman, Kay Dudley later served in the State Senate and numerous party offices and in Governor Frank Keating's administration, Tom Dudley became county chairman, Grace Boulton was later National Republican Committeewoman and state vice chairman, Brake was later county vice chairman, Warren Morris served on the county election board, Nancy Apgar was later county and state Republican chairman, Tom Harris ran for the United States Senate, and Mickey Edwards was later elected to Congress. There were many others to be sure. The leadership of the party that emerged in the early and mid 1960s would serve the party for decades to come.

Kay Dudley remembered, "My first impression of Al was, 'How did this man get so much wisdom about the political process?' I was awestruck at his ability to comprehend the way I felt about issues. He knew how to put my passion into words and knew what to do about it."[9]The teenage Republican organization formed in 1966 included future political stars of the GOP. William "Bill" Price, future United States Attorney, and Tom Daxon, future State Auditor and Inspector, both were later Republican gubernatorial nominees. Al's son, Marshall, later followed in his father's footsteps as Republican county chairman and chaired many campaigns, including Mickey Edwards' successful campaign for Congress. Another active member of the high school Republicans was Mark Tapscott, a future staffer in the President Ronald Reagan White House.[10]

The gubernatorial race was the spotlight contest in 1966. The Oklahoma constitution prohibited Governor Bellmon from succeeding himself, so Republicans were looking for someone to continue their occupancy of the governor's mansion. Second on the list of high priority races was Blankenship's candidacy for attorney general.

House Speaker J.D. McCarty, a strong Democratic leader representing the "Old Guard" politics of Oklahoma, chats with Republicans Denzil Garrison, left, and Governor Henry Bellmon, right. *Courtesy Oklahoma Publishing Company.*

However, the crown jewel of the 1966 campaign was the battle for the District 92 seat in the Oklahoma House of Representatives in south Oklahoma City. The seat was held by House Speaker J.D. McCarty, perhaps the single most powerful politician in Oklahoma history. Because Oklahoma's constitution makes the governor a relatively

BELOW: Al helped recruit mortuary owner Vondel L. Smith to run against Oklahoma House Speaker J.D. McCarty in 1966. *Courtesy Oklahoma Publishing Company.*

weak public official, the Speaker of the House often becomes more powerful than the governor or president pro tempore of the State Senate.

McCarty had served in the legislature for 26 years and ruled state government with an iron fist. He controlled state patronage jobs and brought fear to opponents, except for Al and his hearty band of Republicans on Oklahoma City's southside. In fact, Al recruited opponents to run against McCarty every two years from 1960 to 1964, but McCarty prevailed each time.

In 1966, the registration in District 92 was overwhelmingly Democratic, but that did not deter Al. He believed McCarty represented "everything that was wrong with politics as usual in a good old boy state."[11] A defeat of McCarty could drive a wedge in the power structure at the State Capitol and make giant strides toward a two-party system.

For the 1966 legislative race for McCarty's seat, Al and members of the South Oklahoma City Women's Republican Club recruited funeral home operator Vondel L. Smith. Smith was a World War II veteran and a member of the board of Hillcrest Hospital, active in his church and civic clubs, and had an attractive family, a supportive wife, and three successful children.

Al, along with Gladys Gockel, vice chairman of the Republican Party, orchestrated every move of Smith's campaign. People thought both Al and Smith were crazy for taking on the powerful Democrat in a district where Democrats outnumbered Republicans five-to-one. Smith was a quiet, unassuming man, but his character, personal life, and business reputation were impeccable. His clean look and even cleaner reputation presented a perfect contrast to the smoke-filled rooms of what Al called the "good old boy" era.[12]

This is the only photograph known to exist of the 1966 shoebox campaign, showing workers contacting potential voters by telephone. The phone bank was in Al's personal office at 3215 South Western Avenue.

Smith's campaign was grassroots politics at its best and would be emulated across the country by Republican candidate handlers. The plan was simple—quietly outwork and out organize an overly confident opponent who had not had a close race in decades.

The campaign was dubbed by Al as the "shoe box" campaign because a shoe box became the organizing tool. Al acquired two expensive criss-cross directories that listed every business and residence in the district. Marshall Snipes and Smith's daughters, Marla and Janelle, spent the summer cutting the address listings from the directory into strips and gluing them to a piece of paper by precinct—making a handy list of potential voters in a particular precinct and matching the list against registered voters that had been hand copied from election board records. It was long before computers made possible instant access to voter lists.[13]

Cards with information about residents were filed block-by-block in shoe boxes. In a laborious process, residents were checked by hand against the official list of registered voters in each precinct. The shoe box method gave Al important information about residents who had not yet registered. "They were an untapped source of support," he remembered.[14]

Al recruited an army of volunteers to work the shoeboxes. Most of the contact was made by volunteers manning telephones at Al's office at 3215 South Western Avenue. The phones were active from 9:00 a.m. to 9:30 p.m. six days a week.

It was easy to convince volunteers to work for Smith. His smile and genuine qualities attracted people, especially in contrast to McCarty's image as a political boss. Image became a big selling point in the campaign. On the issues, McCarty was viewed as a spender and in favor of tax increases, while Smith campaigned for prayer in schools and increased funding for old age pensioners and schools. With Al's advice, Smith was also the first candidate to make a junior college for south Oklahoma City a campaign issue.[15]

Campaign workers ideally worked neighborhoods in which they lived. It was Al's theory that volunteers could have influence on people they knew—it was much better than calling on strangers. Workers used the telephone to carry Smith's campaign message to the district. During a contact, the worker would take notes on the 3" x 5" card, listing information about the household.

Al's family also worked in the campaign. Marshall cut his political teeth as a campaign staffer. Rebecca was a little worried about her family during the bitter fight against J.D. McCarty. Becky remembered, "Mom was scared. She didn't tell me until much later, but she was fearful that our phones were tapped and people were watching our house."[16]

The Snipes children folded and distributed campaign brochures. It was a team effort to pick up campaign material at the printer and staple, stuff, and stamp campaign mailings at the dining room table. The children also were involved in calling potential voters to urge them to support Smith's candidacy.[17]

Because he was the owner of the Vondel L. Smith Mortuary, Smith's name was well known. Campaigning by the shoebox volunteers consisted of reading from prepared scripts and mailing follow-up brochures. It was the era before massive television advertising and modern day telemarketing took the personal touch out of campaigning. In 1966, Al's comprehensive plan of neighbors influencing neighbors was working.[18]

If a voter was listed as a "yes" in the Smith column, he or she was asked to volunteer to have a yard sign posted. If a voter was described as a "no" vote or "uncommitted," block workers returned to the prospect's home with more information, all the way to election day. Constant contact was maintained with the "yes" voters to build a relationship and maintain their commitment.

The element of surprise was a fundamental part of the campaign. As Al, through the results of the shoe box effort, saw large numbers of voters begin to express their support for Smith, he believed that the campaign was Smith's to lose. A certain level of paranoia set in and Al decided to keep the results and trends of the shoe box tallies to himself and a few close campaign workers. Al did not want an overconfident team of campaign workers. Consequently, a decision was made to distribute a smattering of black and white Smith campaign signs around the district to make it look like Smith had only normal, sporadic Republican support in a heavily Democratic area.[19]

At this point Al believed the only way Smith could lose was if the election was stolen. Accordingly, he put into place an elaborate methodology to verify that each voter casting a ballot was legal. He also placed challengers at each polling place, armed with a list of eligible voters.

In the week before the election, each voter who had indicated in the shoe box inquiry that he was for Smith was asked to place a huge, bright fluorescent orange, glow-in-the-dark-and-light sign in their yards on the Saturday before the election. Most people in the district attended church on Sunday morning. The idea was to make it look like a light bulb went off in the neighborhoods where shoebox results indicated that Smith enjoyed a two-to-one margin.

There were three reasons why Al waited to distribute the yard signs until the last minute. First, he did not think McCarty would have time to react to the overwhelming display of Smith support. Second, Republicans had problems with their campaign signs disappearing in south Oklahoma City. A third reason was the great increase of signs from the smattering of black and white signs to the overwhelming number of orange signs. It was a gimmick—part of the momentum building process during the final days of the campaign.[20]

As predicted, almost everyone in the district began talking about the overnight disappearance of so many signs. And, as predicted, virtually every yard sign put up on Saturday mysteriously disappeared before church-goers returned home. But the Republicans had the last laugh. Expecting that the signs would be stolen, each household was given an extra sign to store in their garage and place in a prominent spot on Monday, the day before the election.

Al reflected, "I think the signs overwhelmed J.D. and he just gave up at that point." One of McCarty's next door neighbors later told Al that on Sunday morning when McCarty retrieved his newspaper from the front yard, the signs on the street looked like tombstones to him.[21]

Another last minute strategy was the hand delivery on the day before the election of a Victory Celebration Invitation to potential voters, announcing door prizes and reinforcing Smith's stand on the issues. It was a bold move considering the electoral history of the district. In prior elections, election night parties were known as "watch parties," but Al knew Smith had the votes to win and wanted to maintain momentum by labeling the event a "victory celebration."[22]

Then came election day. A massive get-out-the-vote effort was a natural extension of the shoe box approach—one voter at a time. Each voter who had indicated his support for Smith was called and asked if he had voted. Continual calls were made until it was verified that each voter had actually cast a ballot. In the end, the campaign was able to verify that all but 57 of the identified and committed voters had gone to the polls. No doubt the unheard of verification strategy worked. Baby sitters and rides to the polls also were provided to make it easier for citizens to vote.

When the votes were counted, Smith shocked the political world by soundly defeating McCarty, 2,711 to 1,415, a nearly two-to-one margin. The *Oklahoma City Times* called McCarty's defeat an "earthquake" and a "crushing defeat." McCarty would have returned to serve an unprecedented fourth term as speaker. Henry Bellmon remembered, "There will never be another election like it!"[23]

McCarty later told Denzil Garrison that Al had simply outworked him and outthought him in the election. During the week of the election McCarty told Garrison, "Al has me beat."[24]

The *Oklahoma City Times* correctly opined that the defeat of McCarty could change the course of events in Oklahoma legislative and political life even more than the election of Dewey Bartlett as Oklahoma's second consecutive Republican governor.[25] Republicans fared well in other races in 1966. G.T. Blankenship became the state's first Republican attorney general, the state's first Republican labor commissioner, L.E. Bailey, was elected, and the GOP picked up four House of Representatives seats and one State Senate seat in Oklahoma County, two Republicans were elected to Congress in the state, and, for the first time in history, four Oklahoma County courthouse posts went to Republicans.

Political observers saw McCarty's defeat as the single most important sign that Oklahoma voters were moving away from politics of the past. Oklahomans had gone to the polls and stamped their mark of acceptance upon a stable, two-party government. McCarty, a man generally identified in the public mind as a roadblock to meaningful judicial and government reform, was voted out of office. The gravity of the moment did not escape the editorial writers of the *Oklahoma City Times:*

> Out of the welter of events in Tuesday's election in Oklahoma come these clear signals: 1. Oklahomans now more than ever are voting for the man, rather than the political label...2. Oklahomans want good, clean government with reforms where necessary. They don't like the old pork-chop type of politics and they'll vote down those who symbolize it. Shining examples of this were...the stunning upset of the powerful speaker of the house, J.D. McCarty...3. These long-range factors are helping create a two-party state in Oklahoma.[26]

Despite huge gains for Republicans, including the defeat of McCarty, Al did not rest on his laurels. The morning after the election, he was planning more blitzes to re-register Democrats in Oklahoma County. There was still much work to be done.[27]

LEFT: Al, right, and newly-elected State Representative Vondel L. Smith, part of the "Cleanup Crew," pull campaign signs from Oklahoma City street medians after the 1966 election. *Courtesy Oklahoma Publishing Company.*

BELOW: Al, right, and Dewey Bartlett, elected as Oklahoma's second Republican governor in 1966.

RIGHT: Rebecca was active in GOP campaigns and hosted GOP women's functions in her home. Left to right, Mrs. Pete Allen, Alma Lee Keller, First Lady Ann Bartlett, Wanda Albright, Jean Smith, and Rebecca.

BELOW: The Snipes family in 1967. Left to right, Rebecca, Bill, Becky, Marshall, and Al.

RIGHT: The first South Oklahoma City Junior College board. Left to right, Jim Lookabaugh, Al, Jack Turner, Carlton Myrho, Robert Moser, Wes Weldon, and Leon Nance. Myrho was chairman and Al was vice chairman.

ELEVEN

The foundation of every state is the education of its youth.

—Diogenes Laertius

185

MESSAGES OF CONGRATULATIONS filled Al's mail box in the weeks following his engineering of Vondel Smith's defeat of J.D. McCarty. Governor-elect Bartlett wrote, "Your tremendous efforts in the past months have certainly been an inspiration." Senator-elect Jack Short said, "Warmest congratulations to you on the splendid victory." William S. Meyers, Jr., who had been elected district judge, wrote, "I think November 8, 1966, should hereafter be called Al Snipes' Day. I think that if any one person should get the credit for what happened in this state and county last Tuesday, it should be you."[1]

Former Republican county vice chairman Marilynn Harris said, "Al, you have added some feathers to your war bonnet. Congratulations on a terrific victory. You and Vondel Smith will be considered giant killers from now on."[2]

After the inauguration of Dewey Bartlett as governor in January, 1967, Al returned to preparations for the 1967 Republican County Convention. The biggest question was whether or not he would run for a fifth term as county chairman. He surveyed the landscape, and decided to move on to other ventures. When Al announced he would not be a candidate for reelection, delegates elected Edmond insurance man Melvin Gragg as county chairman. Al was reelected Fifth District Republican Chairman, a post he held from 1961 to 1977, 16 years.

Fellow Republicans lauded Al's efforts by enthusiastically supporting a resolution at the 1967 county convention. Political veterans remembered that when Al took over the reins of the county party machine, registration was lopsided in favor of Democrats and the party organization was non-existent. When Al left office, the party had elected its first two Republican governors, its first attorney general and labor commissioner, had defeated J.D. McCarty, and had dramatically improved its position in both houses of the state legislature.

A viable grassroots organization had been built, many new young leaders had become active, the first permanent Republican headquarters had been established and *GOParty Line,* the Republican newspaper had been founded. When Al took office in 1960, Oklahoma was a one-party state controlled by good old boy political bosses—when he left his position, Oklahoma was truly becoming a two-party state.

The resolution, passed unanimously to a thunderous standing ovation of the more than 1,000 delegates in attendance, said, in part:

> His leadership has produced a climate of enthusiasm and understanding in which Republicans work together towards the enlightenment of the electorate and the election of increasing lists of outstanding Republican candidates, and since he has received statewide recognition towards the defeat of the man the Oklahoma legislature designated as Mr. Speaker, therefore, we hereby confer upon Al Snipes the lifetime honorary title of "Mr. Chairman."[3]

G.T. Blankenship remembered, "The energy Al put into the party was essential to our success. Al was a great county chairman. He made something from nothing."[4] Bud Stewart said, "Al was instrumental in building the base that allows Republicans today to enjoy the success they have."[5]

With more time on his hands, Al turned to a pet project—establishing a two-year junior college in south Oklahoma City. Many people were involved in the formation of Capitol Hill Junior College (CHJC), which became South Oklahoma City Junior College (SOCJC), and today occupies a large, visible campus along Interstate 44 and is known as Oklahoma City Community College (OCCC).

In 1965, Al unsuccessfully recommended to the Capitol Hill Chamber of Commerce to make the establishment of a junior college a major priority. At the end of that year, the chamber listed its priorities—building a junior college was number nine. To Al, that meant the chamber supported the idea of a junior college, but it was not a priority. Because of the lack of chamber support, Al made the junior college an issue in the Vondel Smith-J.D. McCarty race in 1966. Even though McCarty was solidly entrenched with the education establishment, Smith's position on the junior college allowed him to make points with voters. It was not the only issue that won the election for Smith, but it was a practical idea that voters liked.[6]

For some reason Democrats, who still totally controlled the legislature, were lukewarm to the idea and had made no effort to support a junior college for south Oklahoma City. Therefore, Smith, as a freshman legislator, had little success in bringing the idea to full discussion. Another complicating factor was that Al was a Republican and the leadership of the Capitol Hill Chamber of Commerce was primarily Democrat, leaving Al on the outside when it came to having a major voice in chamber affairs.

Ironically, the South Oklahoma City Chamber of Commerce is the only group of which he was a member that Al never served as its leader. He was honored in 1988 as Citizen of the Year and in 1992 was elected Lifetime Director. Al's son, Bill, did eventually become president of the chamber, serving as leader of the organization in 1999.

During the 1968 campaign, Marvin York, a young, energetic, and bright Democrat attorney ran against Smith and won the District 92 seat back for the Democrats with a razor-slim margin of 69 votes. It was the first time that Al and York crossed paths.

York had taught school at U.S. Grant High School before attending night law school at Oklahoma City University. Of Al's involvement in south Oklahoma City politics, York remembered, "I don't remember when Al wasn't the head of the party and in the middle of every election. He was recruiting candidates against me. He was the most feared guy on the other side of the political aisle that I ever ran across. Every election year, he was going to be your problem."[7]

York proved Al wrong on one occasion. When the two ran into each other in 1968, Al said, "We'll grind Mike Monroney up just like we're going to grind you up."[8] Al was right about Henry Bellmon defeating incumbent United States Senator Monroney, but York beat Vondel Smith in his re-election bid for the House of Representatives.

However, Al and York strongly agreed on one issue—south Oklahoma City needed a junior college. With York's support, the junior college issue was alive. In February, 1969, the Oklahoma legislature passed a bill that would qualify the Capitol Hill area as a junior college district. The bill, sponsored by Representative L.H. Bengston and State Senator J. Lee Keels, was signed into law by Governor Bartlett. Both legislators were from the Capitol Hill area and were indispensable to the future of the junior college idea. Other legislators who wholeheartedly threw their support behind the SOCJC bill were Senator Jimmy Birdsong and Representatives Ken Nance and E.W. Smith. The junior college would never have been built without the able assistance of the legislative delegation from south Oklahoma City. Without them, the college would never have received adequate funding.[9]

With a junior college district authorized, civic leaders and legislators immediately called for a public meeting to get the ball rolling. On February 19, 1969, Representative Bengston hosted a meeting at which a petition drive was launched. The circulation of a petition to establish a junior college district was the first in a five-step process. Capitol Hill Chamber representative Bill Koontz was chosen to lead the petition drive. Even though Al's energy as a volunteer was embraced by the Chamber, he was not asked to serve in a leadership position of the project.[10]

The second step for making the junior college a reality was a feasibility study by state higher education officials. Upon Representative Bengston's request, the State Board of Regents for Higher Education (State Regents) completed a study that showed there was a need for a junior college in south Oklahoma City.[11]

The petition drive continued, coordinated by David Hunt, chairman of a newly-organized Community Junior College Committee. Al became a volunteer in the petition drive and helped build public awareness of the benefits of a junior college. The *Capitol Hill Beacon* beat the drum slowly to gain public support with many favorable articles and editorials. South Oklahoma City people were excited, although the State Regents publicly declared there would be no new junior college districts approved until a master higher education plan was completed.[12]

Representatives of the Capitol Hill Chamber of Commerce and legislators presented boxes of petitions to the State Regents in June, 1969, asking that south Oklahoma City be designated as an official community junior college district. Southside supporters were again informed that the statewide higher education master plan was not due until November, and all actions regarding new junior college districts were on hold.

Another small hitch developed when leaders of the Oklahoma City Chamber of Commerce, particularly publisher J. Leland Gourley, began talking about a citywide system of junior colleges. Gourley, chairman of the Oklahoma City Chamber's junior college committee, suggested that the Capitol Hill campus be built first. For awhile, talks between the Oklahoma City Chamber of Commerce and the Capitol Hill Chamber of Commerce were held. Meanwhile, the political process continued. Legislators from south Oklahoma City, led by Representative Marvin York, pressured State Regents to allow voters to approve or reject a junior college district.

Representatives York and Nance went to House Speaker Rex Privett and lobbied him to hold up the higher education appropriations bill until Chancellor E.T. Dunlap would agree to authorize a junior college in south Oklahoma City.[13]

The logjam was broken on November 12, 1969, when the State Regents, upon recommendation of Higher Education Chancellor E.T. Dunlap, authorized an election to be called pending the release of a study of the statewide system. That study was completed within two weeks. The election was given final approval at a meeting of the State Regents on November 25. The Oklahoma City Chamber of Commerce jumped on the bandwagon and began to promote the establishment of a junior college district in south Oklahoma City.

Without any organized opposition, the proposal to establish a junior college district was approved by voters in a special election on December 16, 1969. Nearly 90 percent of the voters in a light turnout voted in favor of the proposition. The final tally was 1,017 to 168.[14]

To this point, Al had served in a background role—but that was about to change. The next step in the junior college process was for the governor to appoint four initial members to the Board of Trustees and those four members would appoint another three members. Governor Bartlett appointed two Republicans—Al and Carlton Myrho—and two Democrats—Leon Nance and Jim Lookabaugh. The appointments were made after Al, the former Republican county chairman and current fifth district chairman, consulted with Bartlett about who he could effectively work with on the Board of Trustees.[15]

Al was reluctant to talk about his influence with Bartlett and genuinely wanted the best men for the job. Myrho, the other Republican on the board, had been chairman of the Capitol Hill Chamber of Commerce, was a successful businessman, and had been an outspoken supporter of the college. Al did not know Myrho well. In fact, when the process began, he did not know Myrho was a Republican.[16]

The Democrat legislators purportedly had given Bartlett a list of potential Democrat nominees for the board. Al and Bartlett reviewed the list and Bartlett settled on Lookabaugh and Nance with Al's blessing. Lookabaugh was a well-respected retired educator who had a great relationship with Oklahoma City publisher E.K. Gaylord, certainly a help for favorable publicity. Nance was a retired school administrator. Both Lookabaugh and Nance brought credibility to the board from the education side.

The four appointed members picked Robert Moser, Wes Weldon, and Jack Turner as the final three members of the Board of Trustees. The Democrats on the board wanted Moser, president of Southwestern Bank, and Al pushed for the selection of Turner, president and owner of Turner Brothers Trucking Company. As a compromise, both were appointed. Weldon was manager of the John A. Brown store in Capitol Hill. His political neutrality and business perspective were valuable to the board.[17]

Al believed the quality, mix, and credibility of the seven members was as good as could be expected. Al was appointed for a four-year term, with the other appointees serving lesser terms.[18]

The seven-man board began to conduct the business of building a junior college. The search for a site and a president began. The Oklahoma Election Board set June 23, 1970, as the day for a millage election. At stake was a two-mill tax levy on taxpayers of the junior college district to fund the operating expense of the school. Al was chairman of the Millage Committee to inform voters about the value of earmarking tax money for the project and ran the campaign to get out the vote from his office. The proposal easily passed. The hike in tax for the junior college was significant because historically the voters of south Oklahoma City voted against almost every bond issue and tax increase.[19]

The junior college board worked harmoniously until Myrho announced his candidacy for the Republican nomination for the State Senate seat held by J. Lee Keels. Democrats were already nervous that the Republicans, particularly Al, had too much influence on the future development of the college. Al remembered, "Carlton's running for office was like pouring gasoline on the fire." Even though Al was not involved in Myrho's campaign, the Democrats believed otherwise and the political battles on the Board of Trustees escalated.[20]

Democratic supporters of the college, especially incumbent Senator Keels, were upset that a board member was running for Keels' seat. The Junior College Committee of the Capitol Hill Chamber of Commerce called for Myrho's resignation from the board. The trustees took no action on the request. Myrho lost the primary and never faced Keels.[21]

After interviewing several prospects, the trustees hired Dr. J.C. Nichols as the first president of SOCJC, although there was no physical location or students to be president of at that point. Al had contributed office space for the college until a president was named. The trustees then voted to move to larger space at 5302 South Western Avenue. .

In November, 1970, Democrat Tulsa County attorney David Hall upset incumbent Governor Bartlett and Democrats were back in control of the State Capitol. Shortly after the new legislature met in January, 1971, Representatives York and Nance co-authored a bill that would give political control of the SOCJC Board of Trustees from a non-partisan board to the Democrats. The bill would vacate all seven trustee positions and allow Governor Hall to fill them. Even though the bill never passed, the political fighting over control of the SOCJC continued.[22]

In March, 1970, the first elective board position was filled. Lookabaugh, who chose not to run for election to a full seven-year term, was replaced by Harold Stansberry, executive director of the Capitol Hill Chamber of Commerce. On May 10, 1971, the newly-constituted board stripped Myrho of his chairmanship of the board, no doubt punishment for him running for Senator Keels' seat.[23]

At that same meeting, Dr. Nichols resigned as president of SOCJC, citing personal reasons, although Al believed Nichols was tired of the political environment in which he had to work. Nichols was not certain whether he worked for the board of trustees or Democratic politicians. When Nichols announced his resignation after eight months on the job, Al angrily blamed his resignation on political pressure. Al said, "He is being driven off by political pressure." Al accused Representative Nance of trying to replace all the Republicans on the board with Democrats. Nance branded Al's allegations, "a damn lie."[24]

Trustee Carlton Myrho used the occasion to blast legislators whom he believed were meddling in the affairs of the SOCJC Board of Trustees. Myrho issued a challenge to Representatives Nance and York and Senator Keels to get the bill that abolished the current SOCJC board out of committee, or quit talking about it, "and using it as a threat to satisfy their own desires."[25]

Myrho pointed out in a news release that in the span of 12 months the new board had opened an office, named a president, passed a two-mill tax levy, passed a three-mill levy, employed an architect to design the college's first buildings, and acquired a building site at the corner of Southwest 74th Street and May Avenue.[26]

The next battle came over the selection of a new SOCJC president. Classes could not begin until final approval came from State Regents—and it was well known that Chancellor E.T. Dunlap wanted the board of trustees to choose Dr. John Cleek, an employee of the State Regents, as the second SOCJC president. Al and other board members believed that if Cleek was not hired, Chancellor Dunlap would continue to block the progress of the college and thus delay the beginning of classes.[27]

Buckling to political pressure, the board voted to hire Dr. Cleek, although it was so distasteful to Al that he chose to go on vacation the day the board met to approve the contract with Cleek. "At that meeting," Al said, "control of the college switched from the board to the Democratic Party politicians."[28]

With Cleek in place, money began to flow from the State Regents. Al voted against a tentative budget of $461,429 because SOCJC still had not enrolled its first student. That date was still a year away. Al said, "We're going to have to

At the groundbreaking for the construction of the first building at the South Oklahoma City Junior College were, left to right, Carlton Myrho, chairman of the board of trustees, Al, and SOCJC President John Cleek.

answer to the taxpayers for this." With that statement, the board backtracked and agreed to give more study to the budget. Al had learned that part of the proposed budget was for the hiring of *Oklahoma Observer* publisher Frosty Troy as a dean at the college. Al was opposed to what he considered another political appointment. Al wanted to use that money for scholarships.[29]

In September, 1971, a $5.25 million bond issue was approved for a vote of people on October 26. Two days before the election, groundbreaking for the new junior college was held on the property. After voters stamped their approval on the bond issue, the board went through the lengthy legal process of letting contracts to architects and construction companies, building the facility, opening the school, and managing the bond money. The college was moving forward at an alarming speed.[30]

Classes at South Oklahoma City Junior College officially began on October 8, 1972. Governor David Hall was the keynote speaker at opening ceremonies. After Hall gave credit for building the college to a long list of Democratic politicians, Al called the governor a "cheap politician" and challenged him to apologize for remarks made. Al's comments to a newspaper reporter kicked off a discussion at the next trustees meeting. Al was upset when fellow trustees refused to censure Governor Hall for political remarks made at the dedication. Al said, "I'll just write Hall a letter and express my sentiments." And Al did.[31]

Al was always on the lookout for quality men to serve on the SOCJC board. One example was banker Jim Daniel who was vitally interested in the success of the college located just one mile west of his Friendly National Bank. Daniel said, "Al came to me wanting my views on what the college was all about. He didn't ask me if I was a Democrat or Republican—he wanted me on the board for the pure and right reasons. He was only interested in a great educational facility for south Oklahoma City."[32]

In conjunction with the opening of SOCJC, the *Oklahoma Journal* published a feature story that gave credit to Al and eight other current or former board members for the establishment of the junior college. With a headline, "Nine Men Earn Credit for New School," the newspaper applauded what it called, "an innovative educational system."[33]

RIGHT: Governor Bartlett hosted the Oklahoma County Republican leadership in 1970. Left to right, Dale Crowder; Al, the current fifth district chairman; John McCune, later a state senator; Grace Boulton, later National Republican Committeewoman; Ron Wallace, Oklahoma County Republican Chairman; Governor Bartlett; Thersa Rizzuti; Charles Ellis, a later county chairman; and Ralph Thompson, the 1970 GOP lieutenant governor nominee who was later appointed as a federal judge.

BELOW: Left to right, Marshall, Rebecca, Governor Dewey Bartlett, Becky, and Al at the governor's office in 1970.

great support ... administration
Oklahoma
2-12-70

RIGHT: Al congratulates a graduate during the first commencement exercise at South Oklahoma City Junior College.

BELOW: Rebecca and Al dancing at the party at the Governor's Club in Oklahoma City celebrating their 25th wedding anniversary in 1972.

RIGHT: A photographer snapped this photograph of Al immediately after he learned in 1974 at a meeting of the State Regents of Higher Education that the old board of South Oklahoma City Junior College was being replaced and that the school was becoming part of the state junior college system. Al said, "My only question is how are you going to confiscate us." *Courtesy Oklahoma Publishing Company.*

TWELVE

Still in the Spotlight

Thomas Jefferson said we should
never judge a president by his age, only by his works.
And ever since he told me that, I stopped worrying.

—RONALD REAGAN

NO MATTER HOW HARD **AL** TRIED to just run his insurance agency, his dedication to progress in south Oklahoma City kept him in the spotlight. He continued his service on the board of trustees of South Oklahoma City Junior College as buildings rose on the prairie where the college was being constructed.

The Democrat-controlled legislature made another attempt to abolish the governing board and give Governor Hall the power to replace trustees at will. Such a provision was contained in a bill that sailed through the legislature. Newspaper reporters recognized that Al was the target of the bill. A story in the *Oklahoma Journal* said, "The bill gives Hall the authority to replace the entire membership of the junior college board, along with the boards of five other junior colleges…The most likely target Hall is expected to zero in on is Al Snipes, former Fifth District Republican Chairman. Snipes attempted last year to get the board to censure Hall for remarks made at the college's formal dedication."[1]

However, a joint legislative conference committee struck the junior college language from the higher education funding bill and the board of trustees was safe again.

A month later, in June, 1973, Al was elected chairman of the SOCJC board. Strangely, Al received all the Republican votes and one Democrat vote, that of Leon Nance, the outgoing chairman who had asked him to run. Carlton Myrho, the man who Democrats tried to remove from the board, received the remaining Democrat votes, leading Al to believe that Democrats believed Myrho was the lesser of two evils.[2]

Al's first action was to appoint a committee to investigate the feasibility of SOCJC joining the state higher education system, rather than operate as a locally funded junior college district.

An election brochure boosted Al's successful candidacy for reelection
to the South Oklahoma City Junior College Board of Trustees in 1974.

Al and other members of the board were concerned that
expenditures at the college were "getting out of hand" and that
being part of the state system would ensure a practical level of
accountability. Al had been encouraged to take the chairman's
job by outgoing chairman Leon Nance who had admittedly
failed in attempts to censure college president Cleek for what Al
and Nance believed were exaggerations of student population
to increase state financial aid, excessive staff, and lavish spending. To Al, it appeared that there were more staff members than
students at the fledgling school.[3]

In January, 1974, Al was a candidate for reelection to a seven-year term on the SOCJC board. He easily defeated two other candidates, Lloyd Leveridge and Paul Weselhoft, with 69 percent of the votes.[4]

In March, 1974, Al led the effort to oust Dr. Cleek as president of SOCJC. The board unanimously refused to renew Cleek's annual contract. The Democratic legislators were outraged and demanded a meeting with board members—a meeting that never happened. Instead, the legislature renewed its past attempts of passing legislation that would force SOCJC to become part of the state higher education system and abolish the board of trustees.[5]

For a short time, Cleek did not accept the vote of the board and continued to show up at the president's office, even after the board hired Al Taylor as acting president. Al, as chairman of the board, took matters into his own hands and wrote Cleek, "Since you are no longer the President, will you please return the keys to the college and also the automobile which the college has furnished you."[6]

Again, Cleek stayed, contending the board did not have the right to fire him. Al wrote Cleek again, this time with the additional signatures of the other six board members. The letter said:

> Dear John: For the good of all concerned, we would appreciate it very much if you would remove your personal effects from the college and return the college auto and credit card. We request that this be done no later than 7:30 a.m. April 8, 1974. We also feel that your presence at the college has created discomfort to the staff and students; therefore, we think it best for all concerned if you absent yourself from the college campus.[7]

Cleek still refused to leave. Al seized the president's office and had all of Cleek's personal items removed. Al retained physical control of the office, as Cleek stood helplessly by, until the acting president moved in. On April 8, the board named Dr. Hugh J. Turner, Jr., as the school's new president and voted to join the state system of higher education, subject to approval of the voters of the school district. Al and other board members believed that it was important for the people who voted to establish and fund the college with their tax dollars to vote on whether or not to join the state system which would require the deeding of the property to the State of Oklahoma. Later, it was determined by County Election Board Secretary Tex Newman that election laws did not allow the calling of an election for that purpose.[8]

While the board tried to position itself to be part of the state system, more problems arose. On April 11, 1974, Governor Hall signed into law House Bill 1497. After years of threats, the legislature had passed the bill to officially place SOCJC in the state higher education system and allow Governor Hall to appoint a new board.

On the day the bill was signed into law, Al wrote Chancellor E.T. Dunlap, requesting a meeting with State Regents. Al wanted to delay any final declaration of SOCJC being placed in the state system until the board was sure that taxpayers and students were being protected.

However, State Regents met on April 22 and refused to delay a vote on the issue. To the contrary, regents passed Resolution No. 967 officially proclaiming SOCJC to be a state junior college and a full member institution of the Oklahoma State System of Higher Education. Al was livid, telling a reporter, "State regents have joined hands with a ruthless group of power hungry local politicians to keep education in the dark ages for political purposes." Al called the passage of the resolution a "confiscation" of SOCJC from the taxpayers of the south Oklahoma City school distict.[9]

Within 10 days, Governor Hall appointed a new board. The original trustees who had organized the college, built the facility, and laid the foundation for the college to evolve into Oklahoma City Community College (OCCC), the splendid institution it is today, had been replaced. The battle was officially over.[10]

In one last news article related to the events of the first four years of the college, Frosty Troy took a shot at Al in his *Oklahoma Observer* newspaper. Troy called the ousted president, John Cleek, a dynamic young educator who had been embroiled in agony and ecstasy—agony in attempting to deal with political realities—and ecstasy in putting together a remarkable educational facility. Troy accused former Governor Bartlett of stacking the board with Republicans. Of Al, Troy said, "Heading the list was the GOP rightwing kingfish himself, Al Snipes. If you don't know Snipes, you've missed meeting the prototype of the back-biting politician, a man so far to the right you couldn't find him with a flashlight."[11]

Al considered Troy's comments a compliment, considering the source and the fact that Al had blocked Troy's hiring at South Oklahoma City Junior College.

Even though he was no longer on the governing board, Al was content with the fact that the college was open for business with a first rate physical plant in a location that could expand as the college grew. Later, in Governor Henry Bellmon's second term, Al was appointed by Bellmon to serve on the OCCC Board of Regents. This time, his service was without fanfare. When Al's term expired, Democratic Governor David Walters declined to reappoint him. During his first term in the mid-

A future president of Oklahoma City Community College was a member of Al's youth group at Capitol Hill Baptist Church. Robert Patton "Whopper T" Todd was so close to Al that he referred to him as "dad." Dr. Todd died in 2005. His widow, Marge, said, "Al shared the vision with us of what the college could become."

1990s, Republican Governor Frank Keating asked Al to serve on the board again—this time Al respectfully declined.

Al also was happy about one young man he helped get a job at OCCC. When Robert P. "Bobby" Todd returned from the military in 1972, Al recruited him to work at SOCJC. Al knew Todd well because he had been in the youth group at Capitol Hill Baptist Church where Al and Rebecca were youth leaders and Todd was Lloyd and Marge Bartlett's son-in-law. Todd was the only person Al ever helped obtain employment at OCCC. It was a good decision—Todd eventually became president of the college. In a newspaper interview in 2003, Todd listed Al, Lloyd Bartlett, and Dr. Melvin Todd as his role models in life.[12]

Even though establishing the junior college had consumed much of Al's time in the late 1960s and early 1970s, he did not forsake his role in state politics. In the 1968 presidential election, former Goldwater supporters, including Al, endorsed California Governor Ronald Reagan as the GOP presidential candidate that Oklahomans would most likely elect.

However, the Bellmon forces in Oklahoma clearly favored former Vice President Richard Nixon for the nomination. Bellmon had headed Nixon's national campaign for some time before announcing his own candidacy for the United States Senate.

In January, 1968, Al chaired the nation's first GOP grass roots convention, the Fifth District convention, to select candidates for the Republican National Convention that summer. The Reaganites were in total control at the Fifth District GOP Convention and elected Senator

Al, center, was openly for Ronald Reagan, right, from 1968 until Reagan was elected president in 1980. Al campaigned at local and national conventions for Reagan who he believed could sell conservative ideas in such a way to resonate with voters and get elected.

Richard Stansberry and Gladys Gockel as delegates. Al did not run for delegate and instead supported Gockel. Al was elected as an alternate delegate. Al's longtime belief was that delegates should be picked as a reward for service to the party. Although he could have easily won, he encouraged Gockel to run. It made no difference—both were for Reagan and delegates and alternates had the same privileges and were invited to the same functions at the convention.[13]

Republicans gathered in Miami, Florida, for their national convention, on the heels of the rowdy 1968 Democratic

National Convention in Chicago that had seen anti-war demonstrations and the arrest of the Chicago Seven. Al reported on the convention in dispatches back to the *Capitol Hill Beacon.* He wrote:

> Excitement really began to mount as the Monday evening session opened, but it reached its peak with the standing ovation afforded Barry Goldwater—much to the bewilderment of Huntley and Brinkley in their glass cage above us.
>
> Goldwater did much to set the mood of the convention and bring about the ultimate unity that we felt at the convention's conclusion.[14]

LEFT: Voter registration was still on Al's mind in 1968. This sign was in front of the county Republican headquarters on Northwest 23rd Street. *Courtesy Oklahoma Publishing Company.*

RIGHT: Al at the 1969 Oklahoma County Republican Convention. *Courtesy Oklahoma Publishing Company.*

Al's son, Marshall, was a page at the GOP convention after successfully running the campaign that elected Jerry Fenimore of Woodward, Oklahoma, as president of the National Teen Age Republicans. Marshall became close to the California delegation and became an insider with young Reagan supporters at the convention. Ultimately, Nixon won the Republican nomination, a candidacy that was wholeheartedly endorsed by Al.

In 1970, Al became embroiled in another community fight, the emotional battle over busing of school students to accomplish court-ordered integration. Al had been opposed to federal government intervention in local school matters for two decades—the busing issue was no different. Al was incensed that United States District Judge Luther Bohanon had effectively taken over operation of the Oklahoma City Public Schools by mandating that children had to be removed from neighborhood schools to attend sometimes faraway schools for the sake of integration. The Oklahoma City Board of Education had failed to submit plans that were pleasing to Judge Bohanon—so he took matters into his own hands.

Oklahoma City was sharply split over busing. Judge Bohanon was hanged in effigy—education and community leaders were deeply divided on whether or not forced busing would result in the death of neighborhood schools. No one knew if Bohanon's plan would truly integrate the school system.

Al and Gladys Gockel began organizing opposition to the school district's annual millage election as a protest against the busing of students. Most voters normally did not pay any attention to millage elections in which a handful of voters routinely approved tax millage to provide school funding. Al's opposition to the millage was in stark contrast to his open support of a millage to fund the South Oklahoma City Junior College.

Speaking as private citizens, and not as GOP party officials, Al and Gockel held a news conference in January, 1970, to urge defeat of the millage. Al said, "Education cannot suffer anymore with the defeat of the millage than with this new plan. I am more than willing for my children to sacrifice if it means restoring their right to attend their neighborhood school. The loss of our freedoms can never be restored, but the loss of some time in school can be."[15] School officials had come out swinging in favor of passage of the millage, claiming that a defeat at the polls would shorten the school year. School Superintendent Dr. Bill Lillard painted a gloomy picture of the loss of $15 million in annual revenue.

Al's leadership in the protest brought others to the bandwagon. City Councilman John Smith, said, "I'm not going to vote to give them a dime...As long as the federal government is running the schools, let them pay the bills."[16] Mrs. Richard Gholston, president of the Oklahoma City League of Women Voters, and insurance man and attorney Donald H. Clark announced their support for the move to defeat the millage. Clark was head of a group known as the Neighborhood Schools Association.

The busing issue was close to the Snipes household. His two youngest children were enrolled at U.S. Grant High School in south Oklahoma City and were subject to being moved to other schools to meet the numbers criteria of what Judge Bohanon considered the appropriate combination of white and minority students in each school in the district.[17]

Al and other officials traded charges and countercharges over busing. Ferman Phillips, executive secretary of the Oklahoma Education Association, State School Superintendent Dr. Scott Tuxhorn, and Governor Dewey Bartlett urged passage of the millage. Bartlett, who strongly opposed busing, did not think defeating the financial support of schools would remedy the problem.

Al personally paid for newspaper advertisements that were clear in their message—if voters were against busing, they should vote no in the millage election. In one ad, Al said, "A vote for the millage is a vote for busing, for the cluster plan, and a vote to bus our elementary school children. Money speaks louder than voice or protest. We must defeat the millage until we regain our neighborhood schools at all levels. When this is done, we can vote the money back."[18]

Al took the message to the people—but voters approved the millage on January 17, 1970, and busing of Oklahoma City Public School students became a reality.

Al turned his attention to the 1970 campaign. Governor Bartlett was upset by David Hall in a razor-close election. Al, who had long thought State Treasurer Leo Winters expected political favors by his direction of state deposits to certain banks, convinced Vondel Smith to run against Winters. Al tracked Smith down on a cruise to talk him into running for state treasurer. Al did not believe Smith could win the election, but it gave him a format to raise awareness of the issue. Smith lost and Al lost his seat on the Grant Square Bank board the following year.

Al had been elected to the bank board in May, 1967. Directors of the bank were told in 1970 that if Al was no longer on the board, the bank would receive state deposits again. Doc Smith, director and majority owner of the bank, remembered, "The Democrats had enough influence that the directors were told that as long as Al was on the board, the bank would not receive a penny of state money."[19] Sure enough, "coincidentally," Al was removed from the board and the money flowed.[20]

Bartlett's defeat actually galvanized Oklahoma Republicans. Many Republican activitists, including Al, believed they had let Bartlett down and worked hard to elect him to the United States Senate in 1972.

Bartlett became a favorite of Al's. Al identified with the Tulsa oilman's political agenda, especially Bartlett's continued opposition to forced busing to achieve integration of public schools. When Oklahoma's other United States Senator, Henry Bellmon, voted against a congressional move to limit court-ordered busing, Al led the movement in the Fifth District GOP convention to censure Bellmon. When Bellmon slipped quietly through a back door to avoid a crowd of some 500 parading anti-busing demonstrators outside the Civic Center Music Hall, Al confronted the demonstrators with a loud speaker and reasoned with them to be civil. Later, Bellmon wrote Al and thanked him for keeping the crowd under control.[21]

At the 1972 Republican National Convention, Al tossed his hat into the campaign for GOP National Committeeman, a post being vacated by Bud Wilkinson. The national committee was a 100-person body that controlled the party and dealt with President Nixon on the national level.

Al lost the race to Davis, Oklahoma, rancher Skip Healey, 12-10. It was the only personal loss of Al's political career. Grace Boulton was running for National Committeewoman. Some delegates opposed Al because they did not believe that the National Committeeman and National Committeewoman should be from the same county. Al quickly got over the loss because he believed Healey and he were on the same ideological page—both were diehard supporters of Goldwater and Reagan.[22]

In 1972, Al worked hard for Dewey Bartlett's election to the United States Senate. After the election, Bartlett wrote to Al and Rebecca, "No two did more to win our race than you. Ann [First Lady Ann Bartlett] and I will forever be grateful."[23]

In 1973, Al retired as state Republican committeeman from Oklahoma County, but continued to work harder than ever before to bring to reality Republican ideas for governing. He would maintain his Fifth District chairmanship until 1977 when he chose not to run for reelection. His goal of electing a Fifth District congressman had been achieved with the election of Mickey Edwards—and it was time to move on.

RIGHT: Congressman Mickey Edwards attributed much of his success over the years to advice and counsel from Al. Marshall Snipes was chairman of Edwards' first successful congressional campaign.

THIRTEEN

To Al and Rebecca — Two Wonderful people and two of my best friends — Edwin Edwards

Elder Statesman

*The advice of old age gives light without heat,
like the winter sun.*

—Vauvenarfues

EVEN THOUGH AL'S NAME HAD BECOME SYNONYMOUS with grassroots Republican politics in Oklahoma, he and Rebecca always made time for their children. All three Snipes children were very active in high school athletics, cheerleading, and other activities, and Al and Rebecca showed up most of the time to see them play or perform.

While Becky was cheerleading and in the pep club, Bill was wrestling. "Dad had an uncanny ability to show up just as it was my turn on the mat," Bill remembered. Al sometimes sat in the bleachers at wrestling matches, but more often than not, he watched his son from underneath basketball goals in the U.S. Grant gymnasium. Bill said, "There he had more room to move around and wrestle the matches for us." Certainly no one wanted to be near Al during a match because he was flailing his arms, trying to help Bill make the right move. Occasionally, more people were watching Al than were watching the match on the floor.[1]

Al usually had a Polaroid instant camera with him at sporting events. He used the camera in the insurance business for taking photographs of houses and buildings he was insuring. However, the children remembered the boxes of instant film Al went through at sporting events and other school activities. That explains why so many family photographs of that era are Polaroid.[2]

Al also took interest in friends of his children. Jon House was Bill's friend who played basketball at U.S. Grant. Al worked for hours in the driveway helping hone Jon's skills. Jon learned from Al and is now a coach.[3]

Boxing matches in the Snipes' backyard were legendary. Seldom was there a gathering of boys that ended without Al putting on boxing gloves and sparring with his sons' friends. When Marshall was still in high school, his friends loved to hear Al's old boxing stories and have the "privilege" of going a few rounds with him. Marshall said, "I still remember the look on many of their faces when the high school tough guys would be laying on their backs trying to determine if they still had all their body parts." To Al, it was all fun.

On one occasion, Bill was concerned for Al's safety. After a softball game, the team came to the Snipes' home for hamburgers. One of Bill's teammates, Mel Benson, decided he wanted to box a few rounds with Al. Benson was a big, tough, athletic young man and intent on "teaching the old man a lesson."[4]

However, during the first 20 seconds, Benson charged into three or four stiff left jabs and was suddenly backpedaling. Al, at age 49, took advantage of the moment and began teaching Benson the intricacies of boxing. The young man became a good fighter. Bill remembered, "All the kids who witnessed dad boxing in the yard, or heard the stories, had an appreciation and respect for why Marshall and I always stayed in line." Al was at home with young people and they felt comfortable with him.[5]

Boxing was part of the "rite of passage" for Al's two boys. Mostly for recreation, but sometimes as a method of settling disagreements, the old boxing gloves were pulled out of the closet.

In the 1960s, Al took Marshall and his friends to boxing matches shown on closed circuit television at the Municipal Auditorium. They saw both Cassius Clay-Sonny Liston heavyweight bouts. The smoke-filled auditorium was filled with grown men shouting for their favorite fighter and booing when they disagreed with decisions. After sitting next to Al during the fights, Marshall felt like he had attended the bouts in person. He still remembers his eyes stinging from the cigar smoke and getting an education in four-letter words coming from the audience. Ironically, it was in the same auditorium that Al had many of his boxing matches.

Al instilled in all his children the love for politics and the obligation for public service. Marshall had vast political experience by the time he graduated from high school and began his college years. He had worked long, hard hours in the Vondel Smith campaign against J.D. McCarty in 1966 and had written a document for the Republican National Committee that demonstrated how the shoe box campaign made a difference in the Smith victory.

In 1974, Al was neutral in the GOP gubernatorial primary. State Senator Denzil Garrison, who had teamed with Al as a floor leader for Goldwater at the 1964 Republican National Convention, ran against State Senator Jim Inhofe of Tulsa, a rising star among state Republicans.

At the same time, Inhofe recruited Marshall to be his county coordinator. Inhofe could not convince Al to leave his neutral corner, so he took his son as county campaign chief. Marshall rubbed shoulders in the campaign with many young people who would become important in Republican campaign circles. Bill Price later ran for governor and was United States Attorney for the Western District of Oklahoma. Jack Edens managed campaigns for several Republican candidates and became a well-known political commentator. Joann Barry later became chief of staff for Congressman Mickey Edwards.

Rick Neal was Edwards' chief of staff and member of the Reagan White House. Marc Nuttle was a political consultant to three Republican presidents and campaign manager of the Pat Robertson presidential campaign in 1988.

Other future GOP activists included Rick Shelby, a future state Republican chairman and staff member of the Reagan

White House, and Gean Atkinson, later a member of the Oklahoma House of Representatives and advertising wizard in the campaigns of Congressman Edwards.

Inhofe won the Republican primary but faced stiff Democratic opposition from David L. Boren who had defeated incumbent Governor Hall and Clem McSpadden with the help of the Boren Broom Brigade. Even though Inhofe lost to Boren, Marshall gained valuable campaign experience and began building his own reputation as an organizer and hard worker.

Also in 1974, Al's longtime GOP friend and confidant, Mickey Edwards, opposed Fifth District Congressman John Jarman, a conservative Democrat who had held the post for years. As Fifth District chairman for 14 years, Al had recruited many candidates to file against Jarman, but none had even come close to defeating him.

Al was excited about Edwards because of his devotion to conservative Republican politics and his people skills. With little funding, Edwards entered the contest. Jarman campaigned very little, ignored his opponent, and expected to cruise to victory with the help of substantial campaign contributions from the business community. But, when the votes were counted, Edwards gave Jarman the closest race of his career. The race was so close that Jarman switched from Democrat to Republican after the election, hoping to preempt Edwards from ever running again.

On election night in 1974, Edwards announced his intention to run again in 1976 and asked Marshall to run his campaign. Marshall agreed. Drew Mason was so impressed with Edwards' showing, he signed on to raise money for the campaign. Marshall became chairman of the campaign and Rick Neal was hired to manage the day-to-day operations.

In 1975 Al was reelected Fifth District GOP chairman and began his work for Ronald Reagan, the former California governor who had announced he would be a candidate for the Republican presidential nomination in 1976. Incumbent President Gerald Ford did not excite local Republicans and Al believed the party needed a charismatic spokesman like Reagan to successfully send the conservative movement into the 1980s. However, Ford narrowly defeated Reagan at the GOP National Convention in Kansas City, Missouri.

Meanwhile, Marshall began organizing Edwards' campaign for Congress in 1976. Also entering the race late was former Attorney General G.T. Blankenship. Congressman Jarman had decided to retire, so the congressional seat was wide open. Edwards actually had been running for the seat for three years, but Blankenship's name was well known among Republicans and he would be able to amass a huge campaign war chest.

Al's longtime position of neutrality as a party official became a hot topic. Blankenship expected neutrality, not only because of Al's position, but based upon their long friendship and work together in the party. Blankenship also thought he was better equipped to win in the general election against Democratic frontrunner Tom Dunlap, the son of the popular chancellor of higher education, E.T. Dunlap.

However, Marshall thought it was time to break tradition and asked his father to support Edwards. Al disappointed both candidates, remained neutral, and received letters of complaint from both Blankenship and Edwards. Not to be deterred, Al stayed neutral and pledged his full support to the winner. In the years since, all three of the men have laughed at the exchange of letters and vying for Al's support.

In August, 1976, Edwards' campaign received a big boost with the endorsement of Reagan, who had been defeated at the

GOP convention. Returning the favor for Edwards' support at the convention, Reagan came to Oklahoma City to campaign for the young Republican challenger.

Al's neutrality in the congressional race was tested at the Fifth District GOP convention. As he had done for 16 years, Al ran the meeting with an iron fist, keeping everything on time, with a sense of fair play. But when it came time to determine which congressional candidate would speak first, Marshall asked his father for a favor—let Edwards speak first.

Marshall knew the crowd would be pro-Edwards because the Edwards forces had worked hard at the precinct level to elect delegates to the district convention. Edwards was an excellent speaker and could work the conservative crowd into a tent revival atmosphere—surely putting Blankenship to a disadvantage as the second speaker. Al would have none of the favoritism, and insisted on a coin toss to determine the order of speaking. Ironically, Edwards won the coin toss and Marshall's strategy played out perfectly.

Edwards gave a rousing speech that tugged at the heartstrings of the conservative cause and easily won the crowd—but not necessarily the election. Blankenship became the front runner—popular, well funded, and supported by E.K. Gaylord, publisher of *The Daily Oklahoman*. The race was close. Internal polls during the final weekend before the primary showed Blankenship ahead. In a last ditch effort to win the undecided vote, Blankenship convinced Gaylord to endorse him to seal the election. The newspaper's endorsement was then, and is now, important in any race and has made the difference many times in close races.

But Edwards got a break. The editorial was a vicious personal attack on him, a tactic that in 1976 was not acceptable to the electorate. The editorial criticized Edwards' previous divorce and unmercifully slammed the candidate. Marshall and other GOP leaders offered to pay for a full-page response to the editorial. When the newspaper refused publication, Edwards' campaign officials printed the response and distributed it to every household in the fifth district. The Gaylord strategy backfired and Edwards won the Republican nomination by less than 100 votes. It was an emotional loss for Blankenship.[6] After a recount confirmed his victory, Edwards went on to defeat Dunlap in the general election.

Al finally had someone of his liking as his congressman. He had worked hard to defeat Democrats in 12 elections over a quarter-century span. Now, a friend and co-worker was the new congressman, and the successful campaign had been run by his oldest son.[7]

Prior to Edwards' election, Congressman John Jarman held constituent meetings at the Capitol Hill post office. Edwards decided to continue the practice of meeting with the people he represented, but he held the meetings in his neighborhood congressional office, Al's 3215 South Western Avenue location. The *Capitol Hill Beacon* noticed the change, "Edwards' southside office is in the same building as Al Snipes' office and in fact there is an adjoining door and Al does have a nice big office. Since the TV people require lots of rooms for lights and cords and people, the natural thing was to move into Al's office."[8] Three decades after the 1976 campaign, Edwards, now the director of the Aspen Institute-Rodel Fellowships in Public Leadership in Washington, D.C., reflected on Al's influence on his life and political career:

It is rare that one man can play a major influence in shaping the politics of an entire state, but Al Snipes, by creating the modern Republican Party in central Oklahoma, did just that. Al inherited an almost non-existent political party, organized its precincts, recruited campaign workers and candidates, and almost single-handedly built the organization that made it possible for Republicans, myself included, to win.

It is no exaggeration to say that if it had not been for Al, it is very unlikely that I would have been able to be elected to Congress, or to have had the many other wonderful opportunities that have developed for me since. Many people have helped along the way, but Al has been the one indispensable man.[9]

Marshall Snipes, right, confers with Congressman Mickey Edwards. Marshall chaired Edwards' first successful campaign for Congress.

Even though the 1976 campaign was the last that Al would participate in as an elected party leader, he was far from through with politics. In 1979, he successfully supported a party rule that made it impossible for a Republican to attend more than two consecutive national conventions as a delegate. For years Al believed that delegate positions should go to hard working volunteers as a reward for their efforts for the party. He also believed the positions should not be controlled by party leaders and elected officials—the party workers should run the party and the elected officials should run the government.[10]

Al preached loyalty to the Republican Party and GOP candidates. He also practiced what he preached—he not only supported candidates with his rhetoric, he backed their bids for

After Tom Daxon was elected State Auditor and Inspector, he asked Bill Snipes to chair a citizens group—Concerned Citizens for Accountability in State Government. Bill, right, Daxon and Daxon's wife, Linda, left, at the 1980 Republican State Convention.

office with his checkbook. Tom Daxon, a state auditor candidate in 1978, remembered, "Al was in the audience when I made a plea for contributions at a meeting in downtown Oklahoma City. At the end of my pitch, Al made a big deal about pulling his checkbook from his pocket and writing me a check. He was setting an example for other people. At that moment, I thought to myself, 'Hey, he really understands the fundamentals of raising political campaign money.'"[11]

Daxon, who became the state's first Republican auditor and inspector in 1979, had been influenced by Al since his days as a member of the Teen Age Republicans and in Campus Crusade for Christ. Daxon said, "Al also provided me good counsel. Every time we visited, I seemed to learn something new about him, something that helped me be a better person. Al was probably as tough as anyone I had ever known in the tough business of politics. But he always took the high road, never taking a dishonest short cut."[12]

Al not only cared about the campaigns of Republican candidates, he was concerned about their personal welfare and their families. When Daxon's father, a longtime Democrat, decided he could no longer support the principles of his party, Daxon asked Al to talk to him. The result was that Mr. Daxon was converted, and became a Republican precinct chairman.[13]

The 1978 campaign cycle also saw the rise of another Republican Oklahoma star—Tom Cole, who successfully managed the State Senate campaign of his mother, Helen Cole. Two years later, Cole became executive director of the Oklahoma Republican Party. Later, he was state chairman, was elected to the State Senate, served as Oklahoma Secretary of State, and held significant positions with the national GOP. In 2000, he was elected congressman from Oklahoma's fourth congressional district.

Cole reflected on Al's four decades of working with his late mother and him in Republican politics:

> My mother thought he was one of the most brilliant and able guys ever in the party. He was the quintessential Republican and an iconoclastic Republican. Everyone respected his organizational ability and his tenacity. Beating J.D. McCarty in 1966 gave Republicans the ability to believe that if we could win that race, we could become a majority party.
>
> Al was very successful at making the party relevant and interesting to the press. Al produced results. That was the big difference between him and other party activists. He talked to party faithful and motivated them to get things done—money was raised, candidates were recruited, campaigns were organized, and results obtained.[14]

Al was chosen as a pallbearer at the funeral of Helen Cole because the family knew that she believed Al was the model of personal and political integrity. Congressman Cole said, "We knew that Al never said anything he did not believe and he never failed to do what he had committed to do. Mom thought he had the ability to differ politically and maintain friendships with people that might prove valuable later on when there was a common goal. She said Al was like a fighter—when in the ring he would knock your block off, but when the fight was over, he could be friends."[15]

With the election of Ronald Reagan in 1980, the country finally had a conservative president. Reagan's popularity and the movement he represented had come of age. In Oklahoma, Don

Nickles espoused Reagan's conservative philosophy and rode his coattails into election to the United States Senate. Many other Republicans were elected in Oklahoma in 1980. The state was fast becoming a two-party state.

Even though Al did not hold an official party position, his presence continued to be felt. He took on the role as elder statesman of the party and became the advisor and confidante to dozens of Republican candidates and office holders for the next three decades.

Al's son, Marshall, took up his father's gauntlet for Republican causes. After the 1986 elections, morale was high among the rank and file of the GOP. It appeared that achieving a Republican majority in the Oklahoma House of Representatives was within sight—one of Al's longtime goals. It was fitting that Marshall took on the challenge to achieve that goal.

When Marshall entered the race for Oklahoma County Republican chairman in 1987, several other candidates appeared interested in the job. However, by convention time, all but Marshall dropped out. Al's influence, along with the strong support of Congressman Mickey Edwards, made Marshall's election inevitable.

The 1988 elections were next. With Al's support, the Oklahoma County GOP, under Marshall's leadership, also took up the challenge of taking over both houses of the Oklahoma legislature. Republicans came close to assuming control of the House—five races in Oklahoma County were lost by a combined total of less than 400 votes. The dream of Republicans becoming the majority party in the Oklahoma House of Representatives was still 14 years away.

Al's legacy also lived on through the successes of GOP workers whom he trained in Republican Party tactics. Kay Dudley defeated Marvin York for the south Oklahoma City

State Senate seat in 1986. Dudley was recruited by Al, and remembered, "I could not have won without Al. He gave me all of the knowledge to know how to run the campaign. I had no campaign manager. I just asked Al and did what he told me to do."[16]

Al believed in hands-on politics. "He told us to be sure and touch everybody," Kay Dudley recalled, "He would say, 'When you go to a door, hand them something, shake their hand, be sure and touch everybody—that makes it personal. If you look them in the eye and touch them, it causes them to feel a part of what you're doing."[17]

Even though Democrats outnumbered Republicans in York's district, Al kept telling Dudley that south Oklahoma

City people were conservative and that party registration ultimately did not make a difference. Dudley followed Al's advice to remind voters that she was not an attorney, like York was, and she wanted to help them.[18]

In the administration of Governor Frank Keating, Dudley served as director of appointments and exerted significant influence on the filling of positions in state government. For eight years, every appointment in state government went through her

LEFT: Left to right, Tom Dudley, Kay Dudley, and Al serve as volunteers at the U.S. Olympic Festival in Oklahoma City in 1989.

BELOW: Marshall Snipes, right, confers with former Oklahoma Governor and United States Senator Henry Bellmon.

ABOVE: Al's influence in Republican politics is graphically displayed in this photograph. In 2002, Al posed with a group of Oklahoma Republican elected officials. By that time, Oklahoma had a Republican governor and held all six congressional seats. When Al became interested in Republican politics in Oklahoma, there were no statewide office holders and only one Republican congressman, Page Belcher. Left to right, sitting, Congressmen Frank Lucas, Wes Watkins, J.C. Watts, and John Sullivan. Standing, Governor Frank Keating, First Lady Cathy Keating, Shirley Snipes, Al, and former California Congressman James Rogin.

office—many times with Al's input. "Al was my mentor," Dudley said, "even when his view was in the minority, he stood head and shoulders above the crowd in every aspect of his life."[19]

BELOW: Al, left, donated office space to the campaign of congressional candidate Frank Lucas, center. At right, at a 1994 reception at Al's office, is former Congressman Jack Kemp, in town to campaign for Lucas.

Over the course of 60 years Al has helped dozens of political candidates and elected officials. Here is what some have said about Al:

I first met Al during the Jim Inhofe race for governor in 1974. By this time, Al was already a legend. Al and other party leaders risked everything for the cause in the midst of being in a horrendous minority. It took a lot of courage to do what they did. When I ran for governor in 1994, like everyone else who runs as a Republican, I called on Al for his support. He generously obliged.

—*Frank Keating, Former Governor of Oklahoma*

Al Snipes is one of the true fathers of the modern Republican Party in Oklahoma. He became Oklahoma County chairman at a most opportune time in history. Oklahoma County quickly became the hub of Republican growth, and thankfully we had a leader who was up to the challenge. Al led a historic resurgence that first made Oklahoma County a two-party county, and later extended that new tradition statewide. The roots of the Republican legislative majority that came to power in 2004 are easily traced to Al's years as county chairman. During my time in public service he has been one of the outstanding Oklahomans who have inspired and guided me.

—*Mary Fallin, Lieutenant Governor of Oklahoma*

When I ran for office in 1987, Al was one of the few Republicans who lived in south Oklahoma City I could count on. I am sure he put some of his business dealings at risk, but he stayed true to his beliefs and promoted the

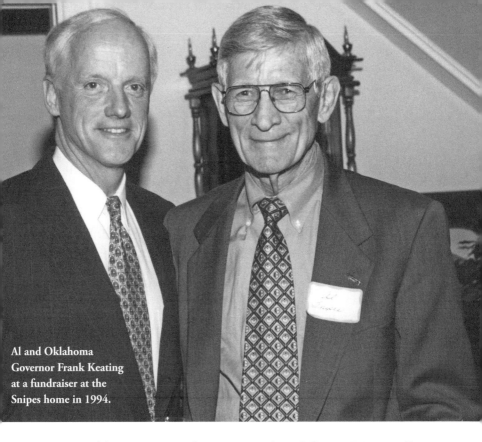

Al and Oklahoma
Governor Frank Keating
at a fundraiser at the
Snipes home in 1994.

Republican Party to become a political force. We can all thank Al for his leadership.

—Ron Norick, former Mayor of Oklahoma City

Al is the heart and soul of the modern Republican Party in Oklahoma. He is the embodiment of selfless volunteer service, and of passionate commitment to the principles of the party of Abraham Lincoln. Al is a conservative who is not harsh or spiteful in his rhetoric. It is his model that has enabled Republicans to gain such strength in the last three decades.

—Brenda Reneau, Oklahoma Commissioner of Labor

Al's leadership helped enable Republicans win races that no one gave us a chance of winning. He brought the organization, planning, and management skills that made him a successful businessman to the party. What Al and others accomplished in Oklahoma in the 1960s is almost unimaginable considering what they did by hand without the aid of computers and cell phones. One of my greatest honors was to present the 2004 Oklahoma Republican Party Ronald Reagan Award, our highest award, to Al. His generosity, leadership, and dedication to the state and nation will be felt for generations to come.

—Gary Jones, Chairman, Oklahoma Republican Party

Al was an Oklahoma Republican when all Oklahoma Republicans could meet in one phone booth. His convictions were contagious. He helped my friend, Kay Dudley, get elected to the State Senate when no one thought she had a chance. The shadow of his influence is long and his friendships are many.

—Howard H. Hendrick, Director,
Oklahoma Department of Human Services

I was a young Assistant Attorney General working for G.T. Blankenship when I first met Al Snipes. G.T. told me he wanted to take me to lunch and become acquainted with two Oklahoma City institutions. One was the Lunch Box restaurant and the second was Al Snipes, Mr. Republican. I quickly learned that most Republican candidates have, through the years, sought his sage and sound advice and certainly his support. His active participation in his community and state helped form the foundation for a modern two-party state and better government.

—Tim Leonard, former State Senator and current United States District Judge

When I worked with Tom Daxon when Tom was State Auditor and Inspector, I always heard about Al Snipes, but was never fortunate to meet him until fifteen years later. In 1996, I met Al at his home and told him I was running for the State Senate. He told me that when I won the five-way primary, to come back and we could talk. I came to appreciate that after my election. After my nomination, Al was in my corner. When my father died a few years ago, Al hugged me and told me that he and Shirley would adopt me and be my parents. I cherish that sentiment and sweet spirit they demonstrated to me that cold winter day.

—Kathleen Wilcoxsen, State Senator, District 45

For many in Oklahoma, Al Snipes is the Republican Party. He is a visionary whose efforts changed a community and a state. I will never forget the day of my first visit with Al Snipes. On July 12, 2000, I decided and announced my candidacy for State Senate in Oklahoma. Within an hour of that decision, Al Snipes had contacted me by phone and pledged to become my first campaign contributor. Since that day, Al went from being my first contributor, to becoming my friend. Much like everyone that Al ever befriended or helped, I am truly blessed to know him.

—Jim Reynolds, State Senator, District 43

When my brother, Jim, ran as a Republican for State Senate in south Oklahoma City, I asked Al, easily the most knowledgeable political person in Oklahoma, to be his campaign manager. The rest is history.

Southsiders do not fight battles based upon whether they will be won or lost. We fight them based on principle. No one has displayed that characteristic more than Al. I can say without reservation that, other than my own father, no one other than Al has been a greater encouragement for me to do what is right in both word and deed, no matter the cost.

—*Mike Reynolds, State Representative*

There is not a Republican office holder in Oklahoma today who doesn't owe Al Snipes a debt of gratitude. Without his untiring efforts it's unlikely there would be a strong, viable Republican Party that could field and support the kind of candidates that have moved us from a single party state to one that gives voters a true choice in the elected officials who govern us. To me, Al was always an icon of toughness, determination and drive coupled with integrity, honor, and kindness.

—*Gean Atkinson, State Representative,*
District 83, 1980-1984

For Republicans in Oklahoma, particularly in the 1960s and 1970s, organization was the key to success. We were substantially outnumbered by Democrats in registration and our only chance of winning was to out organize the opposition by identifying our supporters and getting them to the polls. That basic organization was the hallmark of Al Snipes.

His tireless efforts to establish an effective grass roots organization, recruit candidates, raise money, and motivate volunteers were instrumental in building the Republican Party in Oklahoma and electing its first two most prominent leaders, Henry Bellmon and Dewey Bartlett. Al will always be remembered as one of the true pioneers in Oklahoma political history who helped change the political landscape and brought honest two-party government to the state.

—Don V. Cogman, former Chief of Staff,
United States Senator Dewey Bartlett

At my first state convention 33 years ago, I met Al Snipes and he immediately became one of the standards by which I measured integrity. Of all the people, activists and leaders I have met nationally and world wide, only a few over time remain loyal to their convictions. Al Snipes is one of these. Al Snipes has lifted me by being true to his beliefs. He is that beacon that gives promise to a purpose-filled life.

—Marc Nuttle, attorney and political consultant
to three Republican presidents

I was in my twenties when I first met Al to talk to him about running for Congress. I arrived to meet someone who reminded me of my dad. It took only a few minutes to realize he was a self-made man—no stand on ceremony, but warm, friendly, with a big grin and a man's handshake. He let me know I was not ready to run for Congress but that I should be active in the party and work my way up the ladder.

—Vince Orza, Dean, Meinders School of Business,
Oklahoma City University

Al has led by example. He is a family man, first and foremost. He actively worked in his church and proclaimed his faith. He is unequivocally the founder of the Oklahoma County Republican Party. Al is my hero. At the end of my life, I could think of no greater tribute than for it to be said, "Brian was the best thing since Al Snipes."

—*Brian Maughan*

I have had the privilege of knowing Al Snipes ever since I came to Oklahoma in 1964. He was a great help and support to me when I ran for State Senate in 1965. He is and has been a staunch supporter of good government and I count him as one of my dearest friends.

—*Dr. Tom Dudley*

Al had a tremendous impact on the Oklahoma Republican Party. Without him, and others like him, the Oklahoma Republican Party would not exist as we know it. Al is a leader and an organizational genius with a work ethic to match. His work has transformed our party from a party of candidates with little hope to the party of a majority of officeholders and high expectations.

—*Clinton Key, former Republican State Chairman*

When I became active in Republican politics in the 1960s, we were decidedly a minority party. Today, a strong and growing Oklahoma Republican Party has both U.S. Senators, a majority of our U.S. House delegation, a majority of the State House of Representatives, and hundreds of elected officials in city and county government across the state. This did not happen by accident. Our party sits on a solid foundation built by extraordinary, larger than life leaders like Herb Johnson, Betty Brake, Grace Boulton, and Al Snipes.

—Rick Neal,
former chief of staff for Congressman Mickey Edwards
and staff member in the Reagan White House

Al Snipes was a Republican when we could hold a state convention in an 8' by 10' room. As Oklahoma County Chairman, he was a very hard worker. He helped elect Henry Bellmon, defeated J. D. McCarty, and insisted that those working for him in the party worked just as hard. As a result of that hard work, Al has seen the party from a new-born kitten to a full-grown tiger. He was present at the creation.

—William "Bill" Burkett,
former Oklahoma Republican State Chairman

Al's encouragement meant a great deal to me during my first statewide race in 1988 and at every subsequent opportunity I have had to engage in public service. His wisdom is especially important in times when doing the right thing becomes controversial or unpopular. I respect his integrity, leadership, and commitment. Al gets involved and works hard when he believes in a cause.

—Bob Anthony,
Oklahoma Corporation Commissioner

RIGHT: Al supported every YMCA program, many through direct participation. This photograph shows the first YMCA Indian Guide program at the South Y. Marshall is second from the right on the front row and Al is in the middle of the back row. Dressed in a necktie, no doubt Al came straight from work to the meeting and retired to his office immediately after. Joe Dodson is second from right on the back row.

FOURTEEN

Helping Kids and Families

*To put Christian principles into practice through programs
that build healthy spirit, mind, and body to all.*

—THE YMCA MISSION STATEMENT

AL'S SUPER MARKET & APPLIANCES

TELEVISION — REFRIGERATORS — RANG
FURNITURE — FOOD LOCKERS — GROCERIS

28th and South Robinson
Oklahoma City, Oklahoma

For a long time it has been apparent that one of the greatest needs in caring for the youth of the Capitol Hill Area
has been a Y.M.C.A. program and building right here on the
Hill. The way for us to obtain such a program and building
is for all interested groups to unite their interest and
efforts on this project.

Since such a program is directed toward the physical and
spiritual improvement and guidance of these young folks in
Christian surroundings, this project would be worthy of our
support. It would make possible a system of year-round
sports activities similar to the present "Y" baseball program,
a hobby program, a gym and swimming.

With the object in view of determining how to proceed on
this program, a meeting is to be held in the Ground Floor
Fellowship hall of Capitol Hill Baptist Church, (Corner of
Commerce and South Harvey) on Thursday night, February 12th,
at 7:30 P.M. We urge that you come or send a representative
or delegation to this meeting so that we may know your feelings
on this matter.

Yours for a Better Capitol Hill

Al M. Snipes,
Community Service Chairman
Rotary Club of South Oklahoma City.

FOR MORE THAN A HALF CENTURY, Al has devoted thousands of hours to programs of the Young Men's Christian
Association (YMCA) in Oklahoma City. He became the primary motivator, fund raiser, and visionary for the YMCA in south
Oklahoma City. As a baseball, softball, and boxing coach, and
volunteer extraordinaire, Al poured his life and his money into

developing a first-class YMCA presence in his corner of town.

In 1952, Al approached the leadership of the Oklahoma City YMCA about building a branch on the south side of the capital city. At the time, the YMCA had built a branch in northeast Oklahoma City and Al believed the south side also deserved a branch. However, the YMCA board had just completed a fund raising project for its permanent home on Northwest Fifth Street and the Northeast Fourth Street branch and did not believe additional funds could be raised for a south side location.[1]

In those days, the YMCA was located in downtown Oklahoma City and was primarily a health club for business executives who worked downtown. Al strongly believed in YMCA programs and had participated in membership drives since 1949.

Al did not accept the denial of the local YMCA board for a south side branch. He called the national YMCA office and asked that south Oklahoma City be given an opportunity to establish its own branch. Several days later, Norman MacLeod, executive director of the Oklahoma City YMCA, was in Al's office to discuss the possibility of forming a south side YMCA. Al's phone call to the national office had paid huge dividends. MacLeod told Al, "If you can raise the money to operate a field program and hire an executive director and prove successful for a few years, then we will help you raise the money for a building."[2]

In February, 1953, Al hosted a public meeting to determine if there was enough support in south Oklahoma City for a YMCA branch. Al sent letters to every church, civic club, or other organized group in the area. The meeting was an overwhelming success.

The YMCA was granted branch status on September 21, 1953, and elected its first committee of management, later called the board of directors. Al was elected to the first committee of 24 and has served on the South Board or the Metropolitan Oklahoma City board ever since. Longtime YMCA supporters Harold Stansberry, Lloyd Bartlett, Joe Dodson, Dr. W.H. Stotts, Dr. Alvin Jackson, and K.E. "Doc" Smith joined Al and others in forming the first Capitol Hill YMCA (South Y). Doc Smith said, "Al, Joe Dodson, and I set out to change the image of south Oklahoma City with the downtown business leaders—and we did!"[3]

During its early years, the YMCA operations were conducted from a small three-room house at 213 Southwest 24th Street donated by Dr. W.H. Stotts. Weekend programs were held at Capitol Hill Junior High School which had both a swimming pool and a gymnasium. Al spent many weekends at the YMCA when his children were old enough to participate in the programs. He also was a volunteer boxing coach and taught the art of boxing to many young men. Marshall and Bill took part in the Y Indian Guide Program and played YMCA baseball.

Al was one of the key fund raisers for the YMCA in the 1950s as the program in south Oklahoma City was getting off the ground.

Sometimes when fund raising fell short, Al and other board members had to personally guarantee the deficit. They believed in the programs of the South Y and risked their personal funds to make the project a success.

Al also created a fund raising category known as "sustaining membership contributions." The YMCA primarily sold participating memberships that enabled a member to join and have access to its facilities. Al realized that these memberships would never finance buildings and programs that would adequately serve the needs of south Oklahoma City families. The sustaining member category raised significantly more money from businesses and interested citizens who might never use the facilities. The method was later adopted by the Oklahoma City YMCA and remains the cornerstone of annual fundraising.[4]

From the beginning, Al and other YMCA leaders recognized that a permanent building for its programs must be built. With the help of other board members, Al successfully petitioned the YMCA board for the approval of a permanent building

The first board of directors of the South Oklahoma City YMCA in 1953.

in south Oklahoma City. The condition was that south side YMCA supporters had to help raise the money.

The next step was to acquire land. Curt Thompson, program director of the South Y, and later the north side executive for 32 years, remembered, "We had picked out land across the street from the new U.S. Grant High School, but Al was flustered when he heard the Safeway grocery chain had tied up the land."5

ABOVE: Al, left, and Joe Dodson help install the sound-absorbing tile in the swimming pool area of the Capitol Hill YMCA in 1961. *Courtesy Oklahoma Publishing Company.*

LEFT: In 1962, the Capitol Hill Business and Professional Women's Club held a note burning ceremony, symbolizing the final payment of the group's $1,500 pledge to the Capitol Hill YMCA. Left to right, Mrs. Ben Dodson, Mrs. Roy Lee Jones, Al, and Mrs. Lillie Mae Moore. *Courtesy Oklahoma Publishing Company.*

Al took matters into his own hands and made a visit to the house of the woman who owned the land. He said that Safeway did not have the money, the YMCA did, and that his board wanted to buy the land that very day. The lady agreed and Al arranged to borrow the money from Oklahoma National Bank until fund raising could be completed.[6]

Raising the money was successful. In 1959, Al, Joe Dodson, and Dr. K.E. Smith, led the effort that resulted in citizens pledging 114 percent of the $35,000 necessary to buy the property and planning began for a permanent South Y building.[7]

It took less than a year to construct the building. In September, 1960, Al was proud when the ribbon strung across the front door of the facility at 5325 South Pennsylvania was cut and the South Y had a permanent home.[8] Ironically, Al's daughter, Becky, was the first person to jump in the swimming pool at the dedication.

With a new building, Al was more enthusiastic than ever about building membership in the South Y. In 1962, he was chief of the winning men's division in reaching the Y's goal of 1,000 members. Often, he had the capable help of builder Jim Bowers, who remembered, "Not only was Al a good business partner in real estate, he was aggressive in community programs such as the YMCA. He was always pushing everyone else to raise more money than they thought they could."[9]

In 1964, Al was elected chairman of the board of the South Y, the first of several terms as board chairman. Al was aggressive, almost pushy, about motivating YMCA fund raisers to do their best, to "raise that money," to finance improvements and pay annual operating expenses.

Also in 1964, Al and others devised a plan to get support from banks and

RIGHT: Al was presented the Ed L. Klein Memorial Trophy by the YMCA in 1964. Left to right, Lawrence Klein, Al, Joe Dodson, and Dr. K.E. Smith. *Courtesy Oklahoma Publishing Company.*

other businesses in the area. First, Oklahoma National Bank, the largest bank in south Oklahoma City, was approached and asked for a large contribution. Al was reasonably confident he would walk out of the bank with a large check because his dear friends, Lloyd Bartlett, and Tom Utterback were on the board and were strong YMCA supporters.[10]

Using his good math skills, Al calculated what other banks' contributions should be, based upon the size of a particular bank compared to the assets of Oklahoma National Bank. It was all a matter of math. The other banks could not refuse and wrote their checks accordingly.

YMCA - CAMP CLASSE[N]

DAVIS, OKLAHOMA   Aug. 8 - Aug. 20,196[ ]

It was traditional for the branch board chair to serve on the Metropolitan Board of the YMCA, called the downtown board. Al joined a prestigious group of influential and wealthy business and community leaders such as R.J. Clements, C.R. Anthony, B.D. Eddie, Harvey Everest, John Nichols, E.K. Gaylord, Donald S. Kennedy, John Kirkpatrick, Dean McGee, and Frank Buttram.

The South Y became such an integral part of life in south Oklahoma City that the branch's ten-year anniversary went virtually unnoticed in 1964, except for a *Capitol Hill Beacon* newspaper story that said, "The program has been so successful and active that no one really had time to worry about anniversaries...It was Al Snipes who provided the spark that was needed."[11]

The Snipes family was
very active in YMCA
activities from Little
League baseball to sum-
mer camp at Camp
Classen. In this 1965
photograph, Bill, on the
front row at left, was
attending summer camp.

Al became a hero to many of the young men who learned baseball or boxing under his tutelage. Al truly cared about the boys—not just improving their skills in sports—but teaching them life lessons. He was actively involved in their lives. When one of his teenage Little League players, Robert Barcum, lost his father, Leo Barcum, manager of Langston's Department Store in Capitol Hill, Al intervened.

Christine Barcum had never worked outside the home, had no driver's license, and had few resources to provide for her three children. Al visited the family often and helped them financially. Robert Barcum remembered, "He became my hero because he gave my family the emotional support we needed to get through a very tough time. His kindness made a deep impression on my young heart that made me want to give back to the less fortunate when I grew up and could do so."[12]

Al was reelected as South Y board chairman in 1965 and founded the first annual Gold Card Recognition banquet to honor contributors of more than $250 to the South Y's annual fund raising drive. Also that year, the South Y was presented the Ed L. Klein Memorial Trophy by the Metropolitan YMCA for achieving the highest percentage membership increase among the six Oklahoma City YMCA branches.

Banker Jim Daniel was a YMCA board member recruited by Al. Daniel remembered, "Al was a cornerstone in the community. He was tenacious, but his tenacity had to do with the purpose of the particular campaign he was touting at the moment. He was the 'go to' guy for the YMCA, not necessarily the guy in the limelight, but the real soldier in any effort. Everyone counted on Al."[13]

When the South Y membership exceeded 1,000 in 1968, Al led the fundraising effort and motivated area citizens to support an expansion program that added a gymnasium, locker room, and health club facilities.

Al did not carry the load of developing the South Y alone. The group had a strong board supported by community individuals and businesses. Early and longtime board members were Joe Dodson, Dr. K.E. Smith, Tom Utterback, Dr. William H. Stotts, Dr. R.T. Almquist, Preach Wagnon, Harold Stansberry, Lloyd Bartlett, Dr. Don Hewitt, Jim Bowers, Dr. Alvin Jackson, Joan Sneed, Al Reddick, Gene Moore, and Hazel Jones.

Throughout the 1970s and 1980s, Al continued to volunteer and raise money for the South Y. In 1976 and 1977, he received the Outstanding Volunteer Award for the South Branch. In 1977, he also received the award for the Most New Money. In the midst of his many political pursuits, he used his contacts to promote the South Y and rarely left a business without a Y donation. At times, his fundraising may have overshadowed his ability to bring more people into the process. Al never believed in asking others for money unless he was personally and financially invested himself. As a result, he and Rebecca were generous donors to the annual Y fundraising campaigns.

Dick Lee, former executive director of the South Y, remembered:

Al gets a lot of credit for his fund raising results, and deservedly so. But what sets him apart is his ability to attract people. To continue, any organization must have leadership. Regardless of what he was involved in, Al involved people. He can take pride in the leadership that has been provided by the people he recruited to the

YMCA Board and to membership in Rotary. His "family tree" dominates the membership of the South Y Board and the Rotary Club and I'm sure every organization he has touched.

Al and Rebecca lost close friends and YMCA supporters when Marjorie "Marge" and Lloyd Bartlett died in June, 1979. When Al and Rebecca were first married, they lived in a house on the Bartlett farm. Lloyd Bartlett was Al's banker and confidante in his grocery store days and in the insurance business. The Bartletts had been at the hospital when all three Snipes children were born. The families had attended church together and Al and Lloyd had served for more than 20 years together on the South Y board.

The Bartlett deaths unfortunately made huge headlines in Oklahoma City. Marge had been surprised by burglars in their home on Southwest 40th Street and was beaten to death. A few days later, Lloyd died at home. The Bartlett's son-in-law, Robert P. Todd, was later president of Oklahoma City Community College.[14]

In 1981, members of the South Y search committee were walking one day on a makeshift jogging trail in a small city park near Al's Greenbriar neighborhood. The park, north of Red Oak School between Southwest 104th and Southwest 119th streets on South Pennsylvania Avenue, was little more than a vacant field circled by the jogging trail. Al was thinking about the future of the South Y—wondering if the facility needed to move farther south. He looked around the property and immediately envisioned a new YMCA facility. As usual, he did not let the idea grow stale and contacted Ken McClain, the executive director of the South Y, for help.[15]

At first, the downtown Y would not agree to establish a new branch of the YMCA, but agreed to go along with Al's unique idea to make the Greenbriar location a branch of the South Y. With Al as the chief promoter, citizens threw their support behind a new Greenbriar YMCA branch. Pati Thurman was transferred from the South Y to the Greenbriar location to manage the new branch.

Businessman W.O. "Wendell" Steward and board member and engineer Gene Moore handled all details of buying the land, getting the city to cooperate on building necessary roads, the building, and the adjacent park. Without their work, Al's dream for the facility would never have been realized.

Ken McClain, executive director of the Southside YMCA, right, presents Al with one of many awards received for his YMCA work. In 1987 Al was named Volunteer of the Year by the Metropolitan Board.

When the project was completed, the new branch had a pool, a small activities room, a fitness area, and was home to a complete community program that provided year-round soccer, baseball, and swimming programs for the masses of children who were moving into the area with their families. The Greenbriar branch was timely because of the explosion of new home construction within a radius of a few miles. The Greenbriar branch was only a short term solution because the property was not large enough to accommodate a full branch.[16]

In October, 1983, Al began noticing a change in his health. Always an avid runner, he stopped jogging, complaining to Rebecca that he was always tired. He looked fit, but when doctors ran a series of tests, a blockage was found in the arterial system of his heart, necessitating a quadruple bypass the day after Thanksgiving. No one was surprised, however, when Al was back to work in two weeks and was already ahead of schedule on his exercise program.[17]

Earlier that year, the South Y board had approved a cardiac rehabilitation program under the supervision of Dr. Linda Deere. The unique program to provide local supervised rehabilitation after cardiac hospital care was featured in a newspaper story in *The Daily Oklahoman*. The reporter noted Al's longtime involvement in the South Y programs and commented on the irony that one of the first people to enroll in the rehab program was Al, a member of the board that approved the project.[18]

In 1983, Al was elected to the board of directors of the Metropolitan YMCA, a position he held until he was term-limited in 2006. Ken McClain recalled:

> There was a perception in the early 1980s that had existed for years in the minds of the north side members of the Metropolitan Board that south Oklahoma City was not the desirable place to live. The river had been a

natural as well as symbolic barrier since Oklahoma City's beginnings. Through the YMCA those barriers began to fall. Al, Doc Smith, and Joe Dodson by their participation on the Metropolitan Board were able to project a positive image for south Oklahoma City. Al was a big part of the acceptance of south Oklahoma City. Al gave his section of the city credibility.[19]

As a Metropolitan board member, Al began to push for the formation of an Insurance Task Force to attract a group of insurance agents to secure adequate insurance coverage for all of the YMCA branches. The board agreed and appointed insurance professionals from Oklahoma City such as Bill Livermon, Stan Alexander, Dwight Journey, and others. Many of the members submitted bids and Al was selected by the Task Force to represent the YMCA as its insurance agent. Bill Livermon remembered, "Al used his powers of persuasion year end and year out to the insurance companies involved to expand and broaden the coverage the Y was able to obtain."[20] That insurance coverage would become valuable later.

By the early 1990s, south Oklahoma City continued to grow and change. It became apparent that the South Y and the Greenbriar branch needed to consolidate and move to a new location able to handle the growth. Al and Doc Smith began to push the Metropolitan board to make the building of a new South Y a priority. In Al's mind, the YMCA needed to move its roots further south. The once prosperous South Y branch across from U.S. Grant High School was struggling to break even and was suffering from a long, slow decline in membership and profitability.

In 1992, Al's son Bill followed in his father's footsteps and became a member of the South Y Board. In 1995, Bill was

elected board chairman. Al, Bill, and other board members recognized that construction of a new full-service YMCA in south
Oklahoma City was needed. In fact, Al's continued efforts on
the Metropolitan Board caused the board to name the South Y
facility a high priority for 1995. Then came an unexpected trag-
edy. On April 19, 1995, the downtown YMCA was devastated
by the bombing of the Alfred P. Murrah Federal Building.

Fortunately, more than adequate insurance coverage was in
place because of the work of the Insurance Task Force. A debate
ensued whether or not the downtown YMCA should be rebuilt,
or if insurance proceeds should be funneled to improve facilities
in the branch locations. The debate ended when the Oklahoma
Publishing Company and the Gaylord family, longtime supporters and major donors to the YMCA, donated its former headquarters and significant funds to remodel the existing building
for the YMCA offices. Also, the Gaylords donated adjacent land
to build a new branch in downtown Oklahoma City.

Al and Bill played major roles in the YMCA having enough
money to rebuild a new facility. The downtown facility was out
of date and was listed for sale at $2.5 million. No one wanted
to buy the building at that price. Sam Cerny, chairman of the
Metropolitan board, handled the negotiations on the settlement of the insurance claim as a result of the bombing. In
less than two weeks, St. Paul Insurance Company awarded the
YMCA a $6.5 million settlement.[21]

After the new downtown YMCA state-of-the-art facility
was completed, the Metropolitan board began an assessment
of all YMCA operations in Oklahoma City. A new facility in
south Oklahoma City again became a top priority of the board.
A search was conducted and land at the southeast corner of
Earlywine Park at Southwest 119th Street and May Avenue was
chosen.[22]

The original South Y facility continued to decline and the YMCA board voted to sell the building to a charter school. The branch was officially closed a few months before ground was broken in 2004 for the new facility at Earlywine Park.

The YMCA newsletter in 2004 acknowledged Al's half-century of contributions and support for the organization:

Today, as we anticipate the ground breaking of the next generation of YMCAs in south Oklahoma City...Al Snipes is still involved in making it happen. He's been there since the beginning, and his presence will be felt for generations to come. Al has stacks of scrapbooks... pictures of Al, shovel in hand, at every YMCA ground breaking ceremony since 1952...He is passionate about the YMCA and passionate about his community, and his pride...is evident in the twinkle in his eyes as he speaks about them.[23]

Even though he had passed 80 years of age, Al was vitally involved in the raising of funds to make the Earlywine YMCA project happen. He worked tirelessly to ensure that the Metro Y could raise $9 million to secure matching funds of $1 million from the Mabee Foundation in Tulsa. When the campaign was completed, the YMCA of Greater Oklahoma City raised in excess of $10.3 million, thanks to the efforts of Al and many others like him.

There was no doubt that the Earlywine YMCA, which opened for business in 2006, might never have happened without Al's vision to always improve programs for the children and families in south Oklahoma City. Al's legacy will live on for generations as families swim, play sports, and enjoy the modern full-service YMCA branch at Earlywine Park.

Pati Thurman, who directed the Greenbriar YMCA for many years, said:

Al is a visionary. He looks at where we are and has a vision on where we can improve, and moves us to the future, all the time respecting the history and roots of the YMCA organization. He maximizes resources, encourages, and believes all have something to contribute to the success.

Al is consistent. He exemplifies the YMCA mission to put Christian principles into practice through programs that build healthy spirit, mind, and body. He lives the YMCA mission.

Al is open. He shares his opinion, and even if your opinion differs, it is ok. He remains positive even when life gets in the way.

Al has been, and always will be, my mentor and friend.[24]

Thurman first met Al when she was a lifeguard at Al's neighborhood swimming pool. She began observing his leadership when she was a young YMCA program director, working her way up the ladder to the position of YMCA executive director. Thurman remembered, "At meetings at which I could have been intimidated, Al made me feel at home. He treated me with respect and professionalism and gave me confidence to do a good job."[25]

Mike Grady, president of the Metropolitan YMCA, said, "No one has meant more to the growth and development of the YMCA in south Oklahoma City than Al."[26]

Al also has been involved in the Fellowship of Christian Athletes (FCA) for four decades. He became interested in the organization in 1966 when an FCA chapter was founded at

U.S. Grant High School under the leadership of track coach, Gary Lower. At about the same time, Al's longtime friend, Bob Mistele, took a staff job with FCA in Michigan.

Al believed in the principles and goals of FCA and encouraged his boys to join. Marshall, a high school athlete, joined Coach Lower's group at U.S. Grant and became actively involved in the organization. Lower later became a national regional director of FCA and Marshall served as chairman of the state FCA board and treasurer and board member of the national organization. He also became chairman of the Oklahoma FCA Endowment Fund.

In 1973, former University of Oklahoma football All-American Clendon Thomas introduced Al to Chuck Bowman, the new state FCA director. Thomas and Bowman, who had been roommates at OU, inspired Al to become actively involved in raising money for FCA projects and establishing an FCA adult chapter in south Oklahoma City. As with dozens of other worthwhile community projects, Al went to work. Through his involvement, he met many high school and college athletes whose lives were positively impacted by FCA.

One of the young athletes Al got to know was OU quarterback J.C. Watts. When Watts decided to run for public office, he called on Al for support and advice. Watts served on the Oklahoma Corporation Commission and as congressman from Oklahoma's Fourth District. Of Al, Watts said, "Even though I came to know Al and his political resume when I got involved in politics, I saw him through a different prism. In my heart, he is a man of faith who guides his life by his principles. Character, family, and his love for his country and community are important to him, but it is his faith that drives him."[27]

Bowman said of Al, "He was the perfect fit for FCA. His history in sports and love for Christ made him so. Al and Rebecca

Al, right, attends a 2003 book signing of former Oklahoma Congressman J.C. Watts. Al became friends with Watts as a supporter of the Fellowship of Christian Athletes.

Al and Becky just before her wedding to Ben Maddux. Becky and Ben met at a Young Life summer camp. Even after they were married, they returned to Young Life camps. Becky was a counselor and Ben, a physician, was camp doctor.

often opened their home for FCA functions. The warmth of their hospitality was evident."[28]

FCA state director John O'Dell said, "I was so young when Al began working with me on FCA projects. He made me feel like a million bucks. He told me how great a job I did and how I reminded him of my father. From the very first meeting, Al gave me confidence that I needed. Al made a difference in my life."[29]

Another Christian youth organization that Al strongly supported was Young Life, a non-denominational outreach group organized through high schools. When Young Life came to U.S. Grant High School in the early 1970s, Becky and Bill became involved. Al and Rebecca quickly responded by opening their home for weekly meetings. They were also financial contributors and encouraged their family and friends to become involved. Other adult sponsors were Joe and Charlotte Dodson, Dr. Norman and Gertie Newell, Bob and Mary Hamilton, and others.[30]

Young Life became a model by which many modern church youth groups are patterned. Small discipleship groups called campaigners met weekly. Bill and Becky went on Young Life ski trips and attended summer camps. Becky met her future husband, Ben Maddux, at a Young Life summer camp at Frontier Ranch. Ben was on the summer work crew and Becky was a counselor.[31]

RIGHT: Three generations of name-sakes. Left to right, Marshall, Alfred Marshall "Marsh" Snipes IV, and Al.

FIFTEEN

In each family there is one who seems called to find the
ancestors—to put flesh on their bones and make them live
again. In finding them, we somehow find ourselves.

—AUTHOR UNKNOWN

FAMILY HAS ALWAYS BEEN THE CORNERSTONE of Al's life. From his childhood days in a large family in Cameron, through the Depression of the 1930s, starting a family of his own, and the founding of the Snipes Family of America, family has been most important.

By the 1970s Al's children were grown, had graduated from college, married, and had embarked on their individual careers and lives. Marshall and Bill were certified public accountants with large international accounting firms and Becky was teaching school in Memphis where her husband, Ben, was practicing medicine. By 1978, the first grandchild, Ashley, was born, followed over the next seven years by six more grandchildren, Laurin, Jenny, Marsh, Matt, Morgan and Mandy. The Snipes family had grown rapidly and priorities began to shift.

Al's passion from the time he was young was to build—build buildings, build businesses, build organizations, and build his family. The Buckhorn project represented his passion to build and to provide a retreat where his family could gather for "family time." Buckhorn, the Snipes family retreat, is a 180-acre development located on Lake Tenkiller in eastern Oklahoma. Al and other investors built roads and installed a water and sewer system on the land before vacation homes began being constructed.

Many of the people who played major roles in Al's life have vacationed, met, played, and relaxed at Buckhorn. Some were original investors—Doc Smith, Joe Dodson, Don Lippert, Bud Stewart, Ash Gockel, and Blaine Miller.

All of Al's children and grandchildren grew up spending time in the summers at Buckhorn. Although advertised as a development, Buckhorn was intended as simply a place for family and friends to gather and spend time away from every day life. As the years passed, toys of Al's youth—fast cars and

Buckhorn, the Snipes family retreat, at Lake Tenkiller in eastern Oklahoma. Since the 1960s, Tenkiller has been the favorite spot for family gatherings.

motorcycles—gave way to toys of the lake—road graders, boats, jet skis, and an old jeep all of which provided countless memories for the children and grandchildren.

Buckhorn has been the setting for many events during the last 30 years. The retreat has been host to countless YMCA, church, and FCA groups and many costume parties and political planning sessions. Customers, family, and friends have gathered year round for weekends and holidays. Fourth of July celebrations, Rebecca's home-cooked meals, and visits to the "frog pond" are legendary.

With the children grown, Al and Rebecca turned their attention to their grandchildren in the 1980s and 1990s. The grandchildren have fond memories of their grandparents and are old enough to appreciate their legacy. Alfred Marshall "Marsh" Snipes IV said of Al:

> He is larger than life, his personality, his love, and his shoes. He is more of a mountain than a man. I feel like I'm named after Kilimanjaro. Granddad is a summit of accomplishment, staggering in height. Sharing a name with my life hero has given me a desire for success and a sense of self. His humble spirit and honest heart have made him a champion not only in the boxing ring, the political arena, and in all avenues of business, but also in our hearts.[1]

BELOW: A Civil War costume party was among the social functions at nearby Tahlequah. Left to right, Al, Rebecca, Martha Lippert, and Don Lippert. The Lipperts were shareholders in the Buckhorn development and built a lake home there.

Granddaughter, Jenny Maddux Stenberg, dances with her grandfather, Al, at her wedding.

The first memories of granddaughter, Ashley Kathryn Snipes Harris, were of late night truck rides up the side of a hill in an old jeep at Buckhorn. Al would drive the jeep and sometimes cut the lights off at night and scare the grandchildren. Ashley said, "As I got older, I appreciated Granddad's care for people. He can walk into a grocery store or restaurant and know everyone in the room. He is honest, fair, ethical—a man of integrity in everything he does."[2]

Work ethic, love of family, back rubs, and a drawer of elephant figurines dominate granddaughter Jenny Maddux Stenberg's memories of Al. "He always had words of encouragement for me," Jenny said, "he told me how proud he was of me. I will never forget dancing with him anytime there is music or praying with him around the kitchen table. He taught me a lot about how to love my family, my country, and my Lord."[3]

Granddaughter, Rebecca McLaurin "Laurin" Maddux, is named in honor of Rebecca Snipes, whom she called "Nonnie,"

and Al's mother's family, the McLaurins. She said, "When I think of Nonnie, I think of her life serving others. When I think about how she saved a little money each month from the grocery allowance to save enough to buy a piano for my mom to practice on, or the way she supported my grandfather during countless political endeavors, I am filled with admiration."[4]

Of Al, Laurin said, "His faithfulness and unwavering loyalty are so evident in his life. He loves others with such a passion that one cannot help but feel valued and appreciated by him."[5]

Humility is one of Al's character traits described by granddaughter, Mandy Snipes. "He doesn't let himself get caught up in his accomplishments and distract him from the work at hand," she said, "He is very humble and will down play the significance of his role in any project in the community."[6]

Family time spent at Buckhorn also has left indelible memories for grandson, Matt Snipes:

Careening over rocks and straight through trees we went in the jeep. I honestly thought we were going to die—but we never did. I also liked it when grandfather drove the boat. When we started to water ski and tube, he really took us for a ride. Similar to his car driving, he drove the boat fast and turned sharply. For years, he dressed up like Santa Claus on Christmas Eve. He was always eating radishes and drinking buttermilk. It's all part of his legacy."[7]

BELOW: Matt Snipes and his grandfather, Al, in a canoe on the Illinois River near Lake Tenkiller.

BELOW: Al and Rebecca attended many events of their grandchildren. Here Morgan runs in the Oklahoma All-State track meet.

Grandson, Morgan Snipes, remembered:

My fondest memories of granddad revolve around the holidays. From dressing up like Santa Claus to playing with the grandchildren, he was full of life. He always seemed happier when the grandchildren were around.[8]

North Carolina family reunions gave Al and his immediate family the opportunity to spend time with Al's siblings, 29 nieces and nephews, their children, and grandchildren. The Snipes family from Cameron, North Carolina, had grown to a large number. The reunions that began in 1951 did not become annual affairs until the 1990s. Al decided that because of the size of the family, annual reunions were necessary. Annual trips to Pinehurst, North Carolina, the nearest town to Cameron with hotel rooms, have become a tradition.

Since the 1960s, Al has been dedicated to preserving the history of the Snipes family. His genealogical research began after his father's sister died and left a small inheritance to him and each of his cousins. Al wrote the cousins and asked about their

LEFT: When Rebecca's grandchildren became too old for her to sew their clothing, she turned her attention to making dolls. Many of her dolls won grand champion honors in competitions.

LEFT: The Snipes at the 1994 family reunion in North Carolina. Left to right, Bill, Becky, Marshall, Al, Rebecca, and Becky's husband, Ben Maddux.

ABOVE: The Snipes children in 1994. Left to right, Bill, Becky, and Marshall. Bill, Marshall, and Becky's husband, Ben, had just played the famous Pinehurst No. 2 golf course shortly after the U.S. Open.

LEFT: Left to right, Claire, Grace, Faye, Al, Kitty, and Carolyn at the Cameron Baptist Church in 2000. By 2006, only Al, Carolyn, and Kitty remained alive.

families. Only one responded, but Al was not discouraged. He sent out more than 100 copies of the research to other relatives to ask for information. He logged their stories and their family trees, and shared the information with other Snipes.

ABOVE: The board of directors of the Snipes Family of America in the mid 1980s. Left to right, Elton Edwards, J.T. Snipes, Al, Bob Snipes, Dr. Jim Fisher, and Earl Truett. This photograph was taken in the Snipes Cemetery in Chatham County, North Carolina.

In the late 1960s and early 1970s, Al was a member of the public advisory council of the General Services Administration and traveled several times each year to Washington, D.C. There he found other Snipes family members who were interested in preserving the family story.

In 1979, he met Robert T. "Bob" Snipes who had read Al's family research. After an all-night session at Al and Rebecca's home, the two agreed to form a national organization of Snipes. With the help of Brigadier General James R. Townsend, Elton Edwards, and Joan Snipes, the Snipes Family of America (SFA) was formed. General Townsend, a Snipes cousin, hosted the first meeting of the group at his home in Durham, North Carolina, in 1979.[9]

Meeting Bob Snipes was like "a star falling out of the sky," Al said, "His interest and enthusiasm were unbelievable. Without him, SFA would not be where it is."[10]

BELOW: Al visited many cemeteries in his search for his Snipes roots. In this photograph, Al and his sister, Carolyn, are at the gravestone of Bartlett Snipes Durham, the founder of Durham, North Carolina. The grave was moved to Durham from the Snipes burial grounds on the old home place in Chatham County, North Carolina.

BARTLETT SNIPES DURHAM
1822 — 1858
FOUNDER, THE CITY OF DURHAM

COUNTRY PHYSICIAN AND PUBLIC-SPIRITED CITIZEN WHO DONATED LAND FOR A RAILROAD STATION AND THEREBY BECAME FOUNDER OF A CITY.

REMAINS REMOVED FROM SNIPES GRAVE-YARD NEAR ORANGE-CHATHAM LINE AND RE-INTERRED JANUARY 1, 1934 ON THIS SQUARE SET APART FOR THAT PURPOSE BY THE CITY WHICH BEARS HIS NAME.

"THE MERIT BELONGS TO THE BEGINNER SHOULD HIS SUCCESSOR DO EVEN BETTER."

Al serves as the records archivist of SFA, an active group of more than 600 Snipes descendants who regularly meet and celebrate the family heritage. He organizes the annual Snipes family reunion in North Carolina, including cemetery and old home place tours. He began what is now a database containing almost 57,000 Snipes-related individuals. He authored a book in 2006 about his great, great grandfather, John Snipes.

Bob Snipes, founding president of SFA, said, "I appreciate his deep love of family and family history. In whatever city he was in for the past four decades, he looked up and called any Snipes he could find. Hoping to engage these distant cousins, he sent out hundreds of family histories."[11]

Al's love for passing his family history to future generations is captured in an essay titled "The Story Tellers." In part, the unknown author wrote:

We are the chosen. My feelings are that in each family there is one who seems called to find the ancestors. To put flesh on their bones and make them live again, to tell the family story, and to feel that somehow they know and approve.

To me, doing genealogy is not a cold gathering of facts, but instead, is breathing life into all who have gone before. We are the story tellers of the tribe; all tribes have one. We have been called as if it were in our genes. Those who have gone before cry out to us—Tell our story, and so we do.

In finding them, we somehow find ourselves. How many graves have I stood before now and cried? I have lost count. How many times have I told the ancestors you have a wonderful family and you would be proud of us? How many times have I walked up to a grave and felt somehow there was love there for me? I cannot say.[12]

In 1987, Al and Rebecca went skiing in Utah. Left to right, Al, granddaughter, Ashley, Rebecca, and granddaughter, Laurin.

Rebecca, right, at a book signing in Mississippi with her first husband's brother, Bennie Burril. Al faithfully encouraged Rebecca to write the book and attended the book signing.

Al's desire to see family history preserved included Rebecca's family as well. In 1990, Rebecca, after encouragement from Al, authored a book about her first husband Leslie Burril. After all those years Rebecca was finally able to gain closure to that part of her life.

Al and Rebecca traveled extensively during the 1980s and 1990s. Not only were there trips to Lake Tenkiller and North Carolina, but numerous other trips as well. During these two decades, and primarily in the course of working on Snipes Family of America research, Al and Rebecca traveled to 41 states.

In 1994, Rebecca was stricken with cancer. During her four-year illness before her death on October 16, 1998, Al rarely left her side. Daughter Becky said, "Being with her and walking through her struggles, pain, and misery became his full-time focus and he did it with a spirit of love, faithfulness, and commitment."[13]

Al arranged unending doctor's appointments and hospital stays. When Rebecca was at home, he cut fresh roses from the backyard and brought her countless hot fudge sundaes from a nearby Braum's Ice Cream Store.[14]

LEFT: After Rebecca was diagnosed with cancer, she wondered if she would see her 50th wedding anniversary. Fortunately, the cancer went into remission and the anniversary was celebrated in 1997. This photograph was taken at the reception. Less than a year later the cancer returned and took her life.

FIFTY YEARS – A TRIBUTE TO AL AND REBECCA

On the occasion of your fiftieth year,
Of wedded bliss, and many things dear,
We toast you Rebecca, and Marshall, you too,
For sticking together like fine super glue.

Old Al was a boxer, eons ago;
Winning round after round, dealing blow after blow,
But winning Rebecca was his greatest feat,
With her at his side his life was complete.

Along came Becky, Marshall and Bill
To add to their lives that wonderful thrill,
That only is found in a house, made a home,
By God's greatest gift, new life of their own.

Now time has raced from there to here,
But on the way you've had no fear,
'Cause hand in hand you've walked it all,
The two of you, with God on call.

And for us all you've set the tone,
Of what life's like when you are prone
To give your best from day to day.
That's what we've seen, we're here to say.

And though the years have drooped your lids,
Spread your girth, and aged your kids,
You've led a life, we all can see,
Is just what marriage was meant to be.

ABOVE: This poem was written by
Al's nephew, Craig Clodfelter, and his
wife, Cathie, for Al and Rebecca's 50th
wedding anniversary celebration.

LEFT: Al and sisters Claire, left, and
Carolyn at Al and Rebecca's 50th
wedding anniversary.

BELOW: Al and his sister, Claire, "on golden pond," in the backyard of Claire's daughter, Sarah Watts.

LEFT: Al and Rebecca's four granddaughters at the 50th anniversary celebration. Left to right, in front, Becky's daughters, Rebecca McLaurin "Laurin" Maddux, born August 25, 1980, and Jennifer Katherine "Jenny" Maddux, born June 28, 1982. In 2006, Laurin was attending graduate school at the University of Memphis. In 2005, Jenny graduated from Vanderbilt University and married David Stenberg. She teaches eighth grade English in Massachusetts. Back row, Bill's daughter, Amanda Michele "Mandy" Snipes, born April 17, 1986, and Marshall's daughter, Ashley Kathryn Snipes, born February 8, 1978. In 2004, Ashley married Philip Harris of London, England. In 2006, Mandy was a student at the University of Central Oklahoma.

RIGHT: Granddaughter Mandy in a dress hand-made by Rebecca.

ABOVE: Al and Rebecca and their grandchildren.

ABOVE: Al and Rebecca with grandchildren, Ashley and Marsh, in 1986.

RIGHT: Al and grandchildren, left to right, Morgan, Mandy, and Matt.

LEFT: Marshall and Carla Snipes at their wedding in 1994 at the Hefner Mansion in Oklahoma City.

BELOW: Left to right, Al, Rebecca, Carla Snipes, and Marshall Snipes at granddaughter Ashley's high school graduation

Family 291

RIGHT: Bill Snipes, left, presents his father the Chairman's Award of the South Oklahoma City Chamber of Commerce in 2000. Former past president of the South Oklahoma City Chamber of Commerce, Alba Weaver, said, "As a leader, Al carries the magic within, awakening the magic in others, and makes our community more leader-full and our world more livable."

SIXTEEN

Epilogue

Life is a daring adventure or it is nothing at all.

—Helen Keller

When most people approach their eighties, life slows to a snail's pace, alternating between family visits and frequent naps. But not Al! He continued to be active as ever in political, civic, and church affairs.

After Rebecca's death, Al stepped up his community involvement. For years, he had been the elder statesman of groups of which he was a member. He has attended Rotary Club meetings each Friday since 1949, sought new members, was president of the club, and participated in most Rotary projects, including serving breakfast and ringing bells for the Salvation Army at Christmas. On October 21, 2005, he was presented the prestigious John "Lee" DesCamps Leadership Award for his service to Rotary. He also was named a Paul Harris Fellow and a Rotary Foundation Benefactor by Rotary International for his financial contributions.

Al still serves on the board of directors of the Oklahoma City Community College Foundation. He established the Lloyd E. & Marge L. Bartlett Memorial Endowment Scholarship and Business Lectureship Series at OCCC and served on the committee to honor outgoing President Robert Todd.

In 2000, Al again was recognized by the South Oklahoma City Chamber of Commerce by being presented the Chairman's Award. Al's son, Bill, was president of the chamber and presented the award to his father. At the same annual awards banquet, country and western singer Toby Keith was honored with the Native Son Award.

In 2006, Al served his 53rd consecutive year as a member of the governing boards of either the Metropolitan or the South Oklahoma City YMCA. Many years he served on both boards.

Al served on the Integris Hospital Foundation Board through 2004. He had supported a hospital for south Oklahoma City by participating in the door-to-door campaign to raise money

Dan Tipton, left, was the first administrator of South Community Hospital, later known as Integris Southwest Medical Center. He and Al became close friends over the years as Al served on the hospital foundation board of directors.

for South Community Hospital in 1963. In 1973, Al was asked by hospital administrator Dan Tipton and Doc Smith, chairman of the hospital board, to run a public campaign to determine the governance of the hospital for the future. The campaign was successful. Tipton remembered, "That campaign set the stage for the success the hospital would enjoy in the community. Al was the perfect person to manage the campaign. He always wanted to do what was morally right. He was a man of integrity, and people knew it. Our city and state are a better place to live because of Al."[1]

Al has worked tirelessly in other community and church activities. He served on the membership recruitment committee and helped raise funds for Southern Hills Baptist Church. Until 2004 he was a member of the advisory board of directors of BancFirst, ending 30 years of service on four different bank boards. He continues to manage his real estate business, including his developments at Lake Tenkiller, S&B Investments, LLC, and REALCO, LLC. Al shows no signs of slowing down.

Reverend Doug Melton, pastor of Southern Hills Baptist Church, said:

> Individuals from all walks of life find Al a man they can trust and talk to. He can talk to blue collar workers or sit with presidents and kings and be called upon to give godly wisdom. Al has the knowledge, background, experience, and the trust of others to be an ambassador for our country. But his greatest joy is knowing that he is an ambassador for his Lord and Savior.[2]

Al's longtime banker and friend, Jim Daniel, said, "Al is one of those rare individuals who is more focused on other people than he is on himself. He is a big encourager, and if he senses that there is a cause that is right, Al would be back-to-back, toe-to-toe with every person who volunteered to work with him in the project."[3]

About Al's involvement in youth programs in the community, Daniel said, "I saw his heart for kids through the YMCA. Kids didn't need to have money—they just had to have a need. Al's heart for the future rested in young people. He always wanted to do the right thing at the right time to help kids in south Oklahoma City."[4]

In 2000, Al faced his own battle with cancer. That summer he elected to be treated for prostate cancer in Memphis, Tennessee. Becky's husband, Ben Maddux, a urologist, arranged for Al to be treated by one of his partners. Al stayed with Ben and Becky throughout the treatment period for his 30-minute-a-day treatments. The remaining hours of the day Becky undertook the daunting challenge of keeping Al busy. Becky was up to the task and Al has been cancer free since the treatment.

Late in 2000, Al began dating Shirley Olson. Shirley and her family were longtime friends of the Snipes family. Shirley was the widow of Dr. Forrest Olson, the Snipes family physician. In February, 2001, Al and Shirley were married in a private ceremony attended by their families and a few close friends. Al and Shirley shared the same values, faith, commitment to community, political philosophy, and circle of friends.

The Snipes and the Olsons were anything but strangers. Many of the Snipes and Olson children and their spouses were well acquainted having grown up and gone to school together. Family gatherings at holidays and birthdays took on an air of a reunion, rather than the usual unease of meeting new in-laws. Shirley has been and remains Al's strongest supporter in these later years. When Al and Shirley could not decide on whose church to attend, Southern Hills Baptist Church in south Oklahoma City, or First Baptist Church, downtown, the compromise was simple. They attend early church at one and late church at the other.

Al's life between his 82nd and 85th years reads like the resume of a young businessman and political activist fresh from college. His reputation as "godfather of the Oklahoma County Republican Party" and the "elder statesman" of the GOP in Oklahoma has drawn new candidates to him. He is always quick to provide advice on how Republicans can convey their message to voters.

Since age 82, Al has served as campaign chairman and managed Brian Maughan's campaign for the State Senate. He has chaired both of Representative Mike Reynolds' races for the Oklahoma House of Representatives. He received the Oklahoma

Al Snipes: Fighter, Founder, and Father

ABOVE: Shirley's family at the wedding of Al and Shirley. Left to right, Tim Gregory, Nancy Gregory, Pam Olson, Bo Olson, Shirley, Al, Eric Olson, Debbie Olson, Mike Renfro, and Dianne Renfro.

LEFT: Al married Shirley Olson in February, 2001, at a small ceremony at First Baptist Church in Oklahoma City. At the wedding, left to right, Jim Bowers, Al's real estate business partner and long-time friend, Jim's wife, Bo, Shirley, and Al.

Republican Party Lifetime Achievement Award and the Oklahoma City Young Republican Lifetime Achievement Award is named in his honor. He has been active in precinct meetings and served as a delegate to the county and state Republican conventions. In addition, he has served on the advisory committee to Republican Oklahoma Speaker of the House Todd Hiett.

LEFT: The first Snipes grandchild to be married was Ashley Kathryn Snipes, Marshall's daughter, who wed Philip Harris, of London, England, in November, 2004. In 2006, they began a two-year humanitarian aide assignment in the Middle East.

BELOW: Al served as campaign chairman for the State Senate campaign for Brian Maughan, right. Even though he was 82, Al was at campaign headquarters daily.

Al Snipes has left huge shoes to fill in Oklahoma. His son, Marshall, admits that it took all three of his children to collectively come close. Marshall followed his father's footsteps in politics and business. Bill followed in civic work and the insurance business. Becky, like Al, is devoted to her family. She also has followed

The second Snipes grandchild to be married was Jenny Maddux who married David Stenberg in 2005.

in the footsteps of her kind, generous, and gracious mother.

Oklahoma is blessed beyond measure because a young fighter came to collect a debt in 1946—and never left. Al Snipes' influence on the political, civic, and philanthropic landscape of Oklahoma will be felt and appreciated for generations.

LEFT: Al with granddaughter, Ashley, and her husband, Philip Harris.

RIGHT: Nothing makes Al happier than being with his grandchildren. In front, left to right, Morgan, Jenny, and Laurin. In back, Matt, Mandy, Al, Ashley, and Marsh. All grandsons are attending college.

LOWER LEFT: : Left to right, Grandchildren, Morgan, Mandy, and Matt, and Millie the Dog.

LOWER RIGHT: The three namesakes in 2005, left to right, Marshall, Al, and Marsh at Becky's home in Memphis, Tennessee.

ABOVE: Jenny Maddux graduated from Vanderbilt University in 2005. Left to right, Ben Maddux, Becky Snipes Maddux, Jenny, Shirley Snipes, and Al.

RIGHT: Becky Snipes Maddux and her family, left to right, Laurin, Becky, Ben, and Jenny.

ABOVE: Shirley Snipes' great grandchildren, Jackson, left, and Quinn.

BELOW: Al and Shirley with her grandchildren. Left to right, Al, Nicole, Kyle, and Shirley.

ABOVE: Left to right, Shirley Snipes, her grand-daughter, Ashley Davis, and Ashley's husband, Jay.

RIGHT: Shirley's grandson, Forrest W. Olson, III.

BELOW: Left to right, Shirley's granddaughter, Meredith Renfro, son-in-law Mike Renfro, and daughter, Dianne Renfro.

THE LEGACY OF AL SNIPES

As I reflect on the many friends who have given so much to support our churches, country, and local and state organizations, I am truly honored to have served with them.

—AL SNIPES

AL'S LEGACY IS NOT HIS ACCOMPLISHMENTS. It is true that Oklahomans for generations to come will benefit from better government because of the two-party system. It is true that south Oklahoma City residents will enjoy a better quality of life because of the Integris Southwest Medical Center, the Oklahoma City Community College, the South Oklahoma City Rotary Club, and the YMCA. Those institutions and their successes are the result of the efforts of Al and many others like him.

But what sets Al apart from others is his love of people and the belief in the unlimited potential each of us has to succeed. Like so many who grew up in the Great Depression, Al did not enjoy the opportunities that people have today. His legacy is to leave this place we call community better than he found it so that future generations will have opportunities never dreamed possible a few short decades ago.

Al's legacy is fighting for what is right. Based on the "never give up" lessons he learned in the boxing ring, he knew that what was right was worth fighting for. Al understood that carrying on the good fight, even if he was the only one fighting, would have a lasting impact on the community he served.

Al's legacy is putting one's beliefs into action. By turning ideas into action, he has shown us all that the institutions in our communities that enhance our quality of life and give our young people opportunity are worth our time, energy, and effort. Al convinced us those institutions were worth founding and his legacy reminds us they are worth our energy and effort in the years to come.

Al's legacy is family. Most Americans have a sense of family and a need to be part of a family unit. It takes someone special in each family to preserve its history, traditions, and cohesiveness, to organize the communication between family members, and to encourage the true meaning of family. Al has shown all of us by example how important family can be.

The common thread in Al's legacy is people. His ability to understand that people make things happen and that it takes a lot of people, properly motivated and properly led to change for the better the world around us. His ability to motivate, encourage, and make us believe we can accomplish anything with hard work, discipline, and a desire to succeed has had a lasting impact on countless people in politics, business, church, and civic life.

Al is guided by his faith. His faith in God and his fellow man has guided his life from the depth of his soul. That faith has given him the vision to understand the difference between right and wrong, the ability to fight for those ideas in which he believes, and the tenacity, discipline, and courage to never quit.

Fighter, Founder, Father – the legacy of Al Snipes.

NOTES

One: Southern Beginnings

1. Robert T. Snipes, *Snipes Family of America: 25+ Years of Making Connections,* May 25, 2005 report of the Snipes Family of America, hereafter referred to as *Snipes Family of America,* p. 11.
2. www.barbados.org, the official website of the government of Barbados.
3. www. co.chatham.nc.us, the official website of Chatham County, North Carolina.
4. www.moorecountync. gov, the official website of Moore County, North Carolina.
5. Janet MacDonald Neville and Isabel McKeithen Thomas, *Historic Cameron: A Small Town Reborn,* (Cameron, North Carolina: privately published, 1993), hereafter referred to as *Historic Cameron,* p. 11.
6. *Historic Cameron,* p. 14.
7. Interview with Isabelle McKeithen Thomas, December 15, 2005, Heritage Archives.
8. May 13, 2004 writings of Alfred Marshall Snipes, Jr., in the Snipes Family Archives, and interviews with Alfred Marshall Snipes, Jr., in December, 2005, hereafter referred to as Al Snipes interview, Heritage Archives, Oklahoma Heritage Association, Oklahoma City, Oklahoma, hereafter referred to as Heritage Archives.
9. Ibid.
10. *Historic Cameron,* p. 14.
11. Al Snipes interview.
12. Ibid.
13. Ibid.
14. Ibid.
15. Ibid.

Two: Growing Up Quickly

1. Al Snipes interview.
2. Interview with Carolyn Snipes Gilliam Warlick, July 27, 2005, Heritage Archives.
3. Al Snipes interview.
4. Ibid.
5. Ibid.
6. Ibid.
7. Ibid.
8. Ibid.
9. Ibid.
10. Letter from L.B. McKeithen, July 31, 1941, Heritage Archives.
11. Letter from R.F. Lowry, August 11, 1942, Heritage Archives.
12. www.aafha.org the official website of the Air Force Historical Association.
13. Ibid.
14. Ibid.
15. *The Ring* Magazine, November, 1944, p. 32.

Three: The Main Event

1. Al Snipes interview.
2. Clipping from Hendricks Field base newspaper, July 30, 1945. Heritage Archives.
3. Al Snipes interview.
4. Ibid.
5. Undated newspaper clipping from base

newspaper, Heritage Archives.

6. Ibid.

7. Al Snipes interview.

8. Ibid.

9. Ibid.

10. Bill Tharp, Oklahoma Golden Gloves (Oklahoma City: Bob and Helen Haney, 1991), p. vi, hereafter referred to as Oklahoma Golden Gloves.

11. Ibid., p. 6.

12. Al Snipes interview.

13. Ibid.

14. *Oklahoma City Times,* March 20, 1936.

15. *The Daily Oklahoman,* March 21, 1946.

16. Ibid., March 23, 1946.

17. Oklahoma Golden Gloves, p. 237.

18. Ibid.

19. Interview with Jack McCann, July 29, 2005, Heritage Archives.

20. Ibid.

21. Al Snipes interview.

22. Ibid.

23. *The Daily Oklahoman,* October 8, 1946.

24. *The Daily Oklahoman,* September 4, 1946.

25. Al Snipes interview.

Four: KO'd by Cupid

1. Interview with Bob and Louise Mistele, September 15, 2005, Heritage Archives.

2. Al Snipes interview.

3. Rebecca Davis Snipes, *Let Us Not Forget: Leslie Auburn Burril*

(Oklahoma City: privately published, 1990), p. 42, hereafter referred to as *Let Us Not Forget.*

4. Ibid., p. 53.

5. Ibid., p. 56.

6. Ibid., p. 59.

7. Al Snipes interview.

8. Ibid.

9. Ibid.

10. Ibid.

11. Ibid.

12. *The Daily Oklahoman,* p. 63.

13. Ibid., August 31, 1947.

14. Ibid., September 2, 1947.

Five: The Struggle

1. Al Snipes interview.

2. Ibid.

3. Interview with Rebecca "Becky" Snipes Maddux, November 21, 2005, hereafter referred to as Becky Maddux interview, Heritage Archives.

4. Ibid.

5. Ibid.

6. Ibid.

7. Ibid.

8. Al Snipes interview.

9. Ibid.

10. Interview with Joe and Charlotte Dodson, November 18, 2005, Heritage Archives.

11. Ibid.

12.. Al Snipes interview.

13. Ibid.

14. Interview with K.E. "Doc" Smith, October 30, 2005, Heritage Archives.

Six: Getting Involved

1. Al Snipes interview.

2. www.bioguide.congress. gov.

3. www.multied.com/elections/1952.

4. Ibid.

5. W. David Baird and Danney Goble, *The Story of Oklahoma* (Norman: University of Oklahoma Press, 1990), p. 438.

6. Al Snipes interview.

7. *Capitol Hill Beacon,* May 22, 1954.

8. Mary Lu Tracewell Gordon, *The Republican Party in Oklahoma County,* unpublished dissertation, University of Oklahoma, 1966, hereafter referred to as *The Republican Party in Oklahoma County,* p. 9.

9. Ibid., p. 14.

10. Ibid.

11. *The Daily Oklahoman,* January 31, 1960.

12. Ibid., October 24, 1960.

13. Interview with G.T. Blankenship, August 31, 2005, Heritage Archives.

14. *Tulsa Tribune,* September 22, 1961.

15. Interview with Drew Mason, July 23, 2005, hereafter referred to as Drew Mason interview, Heritage Archives.

16. Ibid.

Seven: Building a Two-Party System

1. Al Snipes interview.

2. Interview with Henry Bellmon, December 22,

2005, hereafter referred to as Henry Bellmon interview, Heritage Archives.
3. Al Snipes interview.
4. *The Republican Party in Oklahoma County,* p. 36.
5. Ibid.
6. Al Snipes interview.
7. *Oklahoma City Times,* June 5, 1961.
8. Letter from Henry Bellmon to Al Snipes, May 15, 1961, Heritage Archives.
9. Al Snipes interview.
10. Henry Bellmon interview.
11. Letter from J.D. McCarty to Oklahoma school teachers, December 25, 1962, Heritage Archives.
12. Henry Bellmon interview.
13. Ibid.
14. Interview with Grace and Don Boulton, November 12, 2005, hereafter referred to as Grace and Don Boulton interview, Heritage Archives.
15. *Oklahoma City Times,* February 14, 1962.
16. Ibid., July 18, 1962.
17. Bob Burke, *Good Guys Wear White Hats: The Life of George Nigh* (Oklahoma City: Oklahoma Heritage Association, 2000), p. 103.

Eight: The Conservative Cause
1 *The Daily Oklahoman,* February 15, 1963.

2. Al Snipes interview.
3. *Oklahoma City Times,* April 10, 1963.
4. *The Daily Oklahoman,* April 18, 1963.
5. *The Daily Oklahoman,* April 18, 1963.
6. Ibid., April 11, 1963.
7. Ibid., April 22, 1963.
8. Ibid.
9. Henry Bellmon interview.
10. Ibid.
11. *Oklahoma City Times,* February 15, 1963.
12. Interview with Mickey Edwards, November 11, 2005, hereafter referred to as Mickey Edwards interview, Heritage Archives.
13. Ibid.
14. Al Snipes interview.
15. Henry Bellmon interview.
16. Interview with Denzil Garrison, December 31, 2005, hereafter referred to as Denzil Garrison interview, Heritage Archives.
17. *Oklahoma City Times,* May 17, 1964.
18. Denzil Garrison interview.
19. Al Snipes interview.
20. *The Republican Party in Oklahoma County,* p. 39.

Nine: The Kingmaker
1. Al Snipes interview.
2. Ibid.
3. Ibid.
4. *The Republican Party in Oklahoma County,* p. 42-43.

5. Henry Bellmon interview.
6. *The Republican Party in Oklahoma County,* p. 43.
7. Ibid., p. 42.
8. Drew Mason interview.
9. Ibid., p. 43.
10. Ibid., p. 44, *The Daily Oklahoman,* January 28, 1964.
11. *The Daily Oklahoman,* January 18, 1965.
12. Al Snipes interview.
13. *The Daily Oklahoman,* February 13, 1965.
14. Ibid., January 27, 1965.
15. Al Snipes interview.
16. *The Republican Party in Oklahoma County,* p. 45.
17. Ibid., p. 47.
18. *The Daily Oklahoman,* February 14, 1965.
19. *Oklahoma City Times,* February 16, 1965.
20. Al Snipes interview.
21. Al Snipes interview.
22. Grace and Don Boulton interview.
23. *The Republican Party in Oklahoma County,* p. 49.
24. Interview with E.L. "Bud" Stewart, Jr., November 19, 2005, Heritage Archives.
25. *The Republican Party in Oklahoma County,* p. 50.
26. Ibid.
27. *Amarillo Daily News,* March 9, 1965.
28. Henry Bellmon interview.

Ten: The Turning Point

1. *The Republican Party in Oklahoma County,* p. 52.
2. Ibid., p. 54.
3. Ibid. p. 55.
4. Ibid.
5. Ibid., p. 56.
6. Drew Mason interview.
7. Bud Stewart interview.
8. Al Snipes interview.
9. Interview with Tom and Kay Dudley, November 19, 2005, hereafter referred to as Tom and Kay Dudley interview, Heritage Archives.
10. Al Snipes interview.
11. Ibid.
12. Ibid.
13. Ibid.
14. Ibid.
15. Ibid.
16. Becky Maddux interview.
17. Ibid.
18. Al Snipes interview.
19. Ibid.
20. Ibid.
21. Ibid.
22. Ibid.
23. Henry Bellmon interview.
24. Denzil Garrison interview.
25. *Oklahoma City Times,* November 9, 1966.
26. Ibid., November 11, 1966.
27. Al Snipes interview.

Eleven: The Junior College

1. Letters from Dewey Bartlett, Jack Short, and William S. Meyers, Jr., to Al Snipes, Heritage Archives.
2. Undated letter from Marilynn Harris to Al Snipes, Heritage Archives.
3. Resolution passed by Oklahoma County Republican Convention, February 11, 1967, Heritage Archives.
4. Interview with G.T. Blankenship, November 30, 2005, Heritage Archives.
5. Bud Stewart interview.
6. Al Snipes interview.
7. Interview with Marvin York, November 29, 2005, Heritage Archives.
8. Ibid.
9. Al Snipes interview.
10. Ibid.
11. *Capitol Hill Beacon,* February 27, 1969.
12. Al Snipes interview.
13. Marvin York interview.
14. *The Daily Oklahoman,* December 17, 1969.
15. Al Snipes interview.
16. Ibid.
17. Ibid.
18. Ibid.
19. Ibid.
20. Ibid.
21. Ibid.
22. Ibid.
23. Minutes of the SOCJC trustees meeting May 10, 1971, Heritage Archives.
24. *The Daily Oklahoman,* May 13, 1971.
25. Press release issued by Carlton Myrho, May 20, 1971, Heritage Archives.
26. Ibid.
27. Al Snipes interview.
28. Ibid.
29. Ibid.
30. Ibid.
31. Ibid.
32. Interview with Jim Daniel, November 3, 2005, hereafter referred to as Jim Daniel interview, Heritage Archives.
33. *Oklahoma Journal,* October 8, 1972.

Twelve: Still in the Spotlight

1. *Oklahoma Journal,* May 20, 1973.
2. Al Snipes interview.
3. Ibid.
4. *Capitol Hill Beacon,* January 23, 1974.
5. Al Snipes interview.
6. Letter from Al Snipes to John Cleek, Heritage Archives.
7. Letter from SOCJC Board of Trustees to John Cleek, April 4, 1974.
8. Al Snipes interview; Minutes of SOCJC board meeting, April 8, 1974, Heritage Archives.
9. *Oklahoma City Times,* April 23, 1974.
10. Al Snipes interview.
11. *Oklahoma Observer,* July 10, 1974.
12. Al Snipes interview; *The Daily Oklahoman,* March 7, 2003.
13. Al Snipes interview.
14. *Capitol Hill Beacon,* August 15, 1968.
15. *The Daily Oklahoman,* January 21, 1970.
16. Ibid., January 25, 1970.

17. Al Snipes interview.
18. Advertisement and hand bill in campaign to oppose the 1970 school district millage election, Heritage Archives.
19. Doc Smith interview.
20. Al Snipes interview.
21. Ibid.
22. Ibid.
23. Letter from Dewey Bartlett to Al Snipes, December 1, 1972, Heritage Archives.

Thirteen: Elder Statesman
1. Interview with Bill Snipes, November 18, 2005, hereafter referred to as Bill Snipes interview.
2. Ibid.
3. Ibid.
4. Ibid.
5. Ibid.
6. G.T. Blankenship interview.
7. Al Snipes interview.
8. *Capitol Hill Beacon,* April 28, 1977.
9. E-mail from Mickey Edwards to Marshall Snipes, November 11, 2005, Heritage Archives.
10. Ibid.
11. Interview with Tom Daxon, November 28, 2005, hereafter referred to as Tom Daxon interview, Heritage Archives.
12. Ibid.
13. Ibid.
14. Interview with Tom Cole, November 12, 2005, Heritage

Archives.
15 Ibid.
16. Interview with Kay Dudley, November 5, 2005, Heritage Archives.
17. Tom and Kay Dudley interview.
18. Ibid.
19. Ibid.

Fourteen: Helping Kids and Families
1. Al Snipes interview.
2. Ibid.
3. Interview with K.E. "Doc" Smith, November 19, 2005, Heritage Archives.
4. Ibid.
5. Interview with Curt Thompson, February 15, 2005, Heritage Archives.
6 Ibid.
7. Al Snipes interview.
8. *Capitol Hill Beacon,* September 8, 1960.
9. Interview with Jim Bowers, November 15, 2005, Heritage Archives.
10. Ibid.
11. *Capitol Hill Beacon,* January 30, 1964.
12. Interview with Robert Barcum, December 30, 2005, Heritage Archives.
13. Jim Daniel interview.
14. Al Snipes interview.
15. Ibid.
16. Ibid.
17. Ibid.
18. *The Daily Oklahoman,* December 18, 1984.
19. Interview with Ken McClain, January 6, 2006, Heritage

Archives.
20. Interview with Bill Livermon, January 7, 2006, Heritage Archives.
21 Al Snipes interview.
22. Ibid.
23. *YMCA Heritage,* May, 2003.
24. Letter from Pati Thurman to Marshall Snipes, December 29, 2005, Heritage Archives.
25. Ibid.
26. E-mail from Mike Grady to Marshall Snipes, January 9, 2006, Heritage Archives.
27. Interview with J.C. Watts, January 5, 2006, Heritage Archives.
28. Letter from Chuck Bowman to Marshall Snipes, December 27, 2005, Heritage Archives.
29. Letter from John O'Dell to Marshall Snipes, December 27, 2005, Heritage Archives.
30. Letters from Bill Snipes and Becky Snipes Maddux, January 2, 2006, Heritage Archives.
31. Ibid.

Fifteen: Family
1. Interview with Dan Tipton, December 7, 2005, Heritage Archives.
2. Letter from Doug Melton to Marshall

Snipes, January 8, 2006,
Heritage Archives.
3. Jim Daniel interview.
4. Ibid.

Sixteen: Epilogue

1. E-mail from Alfred
Marshal Snipes IV,
December 1, 2005,
Heritage Archives.
2. E-mail from Ashley
Kathryn Snipes Harris,
December 3, 2005,
Heritage Archives.
3. E-mail from Jenny
Maddux Stenberg,
December 3, 2005,
Heritage Archives.
4. E-mail from Rebecca
McLaurin Maddux,
December 5, 2005,
Heritage Archives.
5. Ibid.
6. E-mail from Mandy
Snipes, December 6,
2005, Heritage Archives.
7. E-mail from Matt
Snipes, December 6,
2005, Heritage Archives.
8. E-mail from Morgan
Snipes, January 3, 2006,
Heritage Archives.
9. Al Snipes interview.
10. Ibid.
11. E-mail from Robert
T. "Bob" Snipes to
Marshall Snipes,
November 28, 2005,
Heritage Archives.
12. "The Story Tellers,"
author unknown, from
the files of Al Snipes,
Heritage Archives.
13. Becky Maddux inter-
view.
14. Ibid.

INDEX